seling attitudes and applies the approaches of humanistic psychology to Christian spirituality. The process of religious counseling differs radically from personality counseling and psychotherapy. Although the counselor can profit from some of the approaches used by these two professions, the book explains his function and tells him when to refer a counselee to the psychological expert.

With its emphasis on understanding the counselee, much of the material in Father Vaughan's book is devoted to what it means for a counselor to understand another human being. Some of its major topics are: *Approaches to Counseling, The Nature of Religious Counseling, Values in Religious Counseling, The Counselor as a Person, Feelings and Emotions, Needs of the Counselee,* and *The Abnormal Person.*

RICHARD P. VAUGHAN, S.J., is Dean of the College of Arts and Sciences and Professor of Psychology, University of San Francisco. He received his Ph.D. from Fordham University and is a member of the American Psychological Association. His published works include *Mental Illness and the Religious Life,* as well as numerous articles for religious publications and clinical psychology journals.

An Introduction to
Religious Counseling

An Introduction to
Religious Counseling:

PRENTICE-HALL, INC., ENGLEWOOD CLIFFS, NEW JERSEY

RICHARD P. VAUGHAN, S.J.
University of San Francisco

A Christian
Humanistic Approach

1. Pastoral Counseling.
2. Humanistic counseling

An Introduction to Religious Counseling: A Christian Humanistic Approach
by Richard P. Vaughan, S.J.

© 1969 by *Prentice-Hall, Inc.*, Englewood Cliffs, N.J.

13–495283–9

Library of Congress Catalog Card Number: 74–86957
Printed in the United States of America
Current Printing (last number):
10 9 8 7 6 5 4 3 2 1

Nihil Obstat
  Donnell A. Walsh, J.C.D.
  Censor Deputatus

Imprimatur
  ✠ Joseph T. McGucken, S.T.D.
    Archbishop of San Francisco
April 10, 1969

Prentice-Hall International, Inc., London
Prentice-Hall of Australia, Pty. Ltd., Sydney
Prentice-Hall of Canada, Ltd., Toronto
Prentice-Hall of India (Private) Ltd., New Delhi
Prentice-Hall of Japan, Inc., Tokyo

Preface

The purpose of this book is to help pastors, chaplains, and others engaged in religious counseling become more proficient. It is meant to serve both as an introduction to those just entering the field and as a source of new ideas for experienced counselors seeking to improve their skills. At times the approach presented may seem oversimplified and overgeneralized, but this is intentional. It was done to assure the reader a clear initial understanding of the counselor's purpose and his method of accomplishing that purpose. In order to do this, a certain amount of precision and depth had to be sacrificed. In addition, experience has taught me that the clergy as a group is an overworked lot whose reading hours are limited. Many can find the time to read a short, uncomplicated book but seldom manage to finish a detailed, scholarly work.

The central theme is that religious counseling is a special type of dialogue—on a par with vocational, marital, and rehabilitational counseling—whose effectiveness can be enhanced by the use of certain psychological findings. Yet religious counseling is neither psychotherapy nor psychological counseling. Its processes differ radically from those practiced by the psychiatrist or the clinical psychologist. The religious counselor, however, can profit from some of the approaches used by these professions.

Good counseling, no matter what form it takes, requires an understanding of the counselee. The more fully the counselee is understood, the more likely it is that the counseling will be successful. Many of the pages in this book, therefore, are devoted to helping the religious counselor discover what it means to understand another human being.

Some may object to the use of the word "counseling" when is it applied to a procedure that may at times be directive or even instructional. But the theories on counseling range from nondirectiveness to authoritarianism. It really does not make too much difference what name one gives to the special process of communication between the clergyman and the individual seeking his help—as long as the nature, scope, and goals of the process are clearly defined.

This book is the outcome of parochial experience, training in clinical psychology, and insights gained from conducting workshops in pastoral psychology. I have attempted to relate all three in the hope of offering a balanced, effective counseling approach. Although the frame of reference and most of the examples used are drawn from a Catholic setting, it is hoped that what has been said will be valuable to clergymen of all Christian groups. During the past six or seven years, we have witnessed great strides in ecumenism. The churches, instead of working in opposition to one another, as often happened in the past, have now joined hands—at least in those areas where a common effort is feasible. Religious counseling is one of them.

Basic to the theory behind this work is the supposition that God is a personal God who intervenes in the everyday lives of men. Unless one understands and accepts that view, much of what follows will have little meaning.

In assembling this material, I have relied greatly upon my experiences in conducting workshops in pastoral psychology. I am therefore deeply indebted to the many priests and ministers who participated in these undertakings. I am particularly thankful to Reverend Joseph Caldwell, S. J., for his key contributions in some of the chapters. I also owe a special expression of gratitude to John Meany, Ph.D., Carroll Brodsky, M.D., Michael Khlentzos, M.D., Michael E. Cavanagh, Ph.D., and to Reverend Francis J. Buckley, S.J., for his theological insights.

R. P. V.

Contents

vii

10
Needs of the Counselee

11
The Abnormal Person

An Introduction to
Religious Counseling

1

Introduction

Counseling consists of a dialogue between two people, a counselor and another person whom we shall call a "counselee." It is both a science and an art; it derives many of its techniques from the research and clinical experience of psychologists, but it depends also upon the personality, intuition, and insight of the counselor. The art of counseling has a long tradition. In the ancient world it was practiced by the elder statesman, the trusted friend, and the honored father. In the Christian era counseling became a special prerogative of the spiritual father, the clergyman, who served as counselor for the members of his congregation. Only during the past fifty years, with the advent of modern psychology, has counseling assumed the status of a science. The profession of counseling resulted from the application of scientific methodology to a special type of dialogue.

Until quite recently scientific techniques were not applied to religious counseling, as they were to vocational, marriage, and personality counseling. Many clergymen, even those who have received their training within the past decade, have had little exposure to the findings of contemporary psychology. This book has been written for those priests and ministers who may have had a course or two in psychology at the seminary but have not had much formal training in the theory and methods of counseling. It is also

1

intended for the seminarian who is beginning pastoral theology and for the religious sisters and brothers who counsel in parochial schools. For the sake of brevity we shall refer to the religious counselor as a clergyman, but we have in mind readers from all walks of religious life.

Objectives

The aim of this book is to acquaint beginners and untrained though experienced counselors with some fundamental concepts and findings of contemporary counseling theory and to link these findings to religious counseling. For the seminarian or young clergyman the book should serve as an orientation to the science of counseling and as an incentive for further study about the relevance of this science to his own work. The following chapters should also offer the experienced religious counselor with little formal training new perspectives and further dimensions which will perhaps heighten his effectiveness. We have striven for brevity and simplicity, steering away from technical terms as far as possible, or, when necessary, explaining them in the language of the nonprofessional. If oversimplification and overgeneralization occur in places, it is because we have concentrated on giving the reader a clear initial understanding of what the counselor tries to accomplish and how he goes about his task.

In fulfilling the aim of this book we shall try to establish certain attitudes toward the process of religious counseling rather than to supply a variety of techniques and procedures. Good counseling is the product of a theoretical approach—or combination of approaches—and considerable experience. Counseling theories are abundant, and no single theory or technique can be followed rigidly in every case; the choice depends on the personality of the counselor and the demands of the particular situation. Although we have stressed the client-centered approach, we by no means espouse it as the only effective one. Certain situations may call for a more direct or rational approach. It is hoped that the reader will test the views presented in the following pages and determine their value for his own method of counseling.

Humanistic Psychology and the Religious Dimension

Religious counseling differs from other forms of counseling in that its primary focus is on the religious dimension. The counselor is aware of two realities: God and man. He accepts a transcendental God as Father. If he is a Christian, he accepts the person of Jesus Christ as Lord and Savior; he acknowledges the continuing influence of the Risen Savior in the life of the Church and of each Christian; and he believes in the Spirit and Its continuing manifestations in the world. These beliefs influence his actions as a counselor.

The counselee's belief in God and his experiential awareness of the part He plays in his life are also important. Like most people he has developed religious attitudes, values, and beliefs as an integral part of his personality. These factors influence his way of looking at the matter he wants to discuss, and they can help or hinder him as he and the religious counselor work their way through the problem.

Psychology as a science is less than a hundred years old; as a form of treatment for the mentally ill, it is even younger. It has grown rapidly and passed through periods when one approach to the study of human behavior has been stressed at the expense of others. At one time psychology was part of philosophy.[1] When the split occurred, it was thought necessary to sever the umbilical cord once and for all and to follow a scientific methodology. As a result psychologists focused on small quantitative aspects of behavior in the manner of physicists and chemists. Much of what is human in man was lost in the process. Psychologists, having concentrated on the study of such phenomena as vision, perception, emotional reactions, and learning, tried to follow the same procedure when they described personality. They divided it into discrete, measurable characteristics and lost sight of the natural unity of the person. The "self" which everyone experiences as the focal point of reality was fragmented into a number of processes. "The existence of the real 'I' while not denied went by default."[2] Advocates of this method defended it by citing the complexity of man and the resistance of the human personality to rigorous scientific investigation.

In the past decade a new group, sometimes referred to as the humanistic psychologists, has revolted against this depersonalization of psychology. The approach of this group is characterized by a major effort to restore the human element to psychology. Krutch has described the humanist as "anyone who rejects the attempt to describe or account for man wholly on the basis of physics, chemistry, and animal behavior. He is anyone who believes that will, reason, and purpose are real and significant; that value and justice are aspects of reality called good and evil and rest upon a foundation other than custom." [3] The humanistic psychologist gives his attention to such topics as freedom and responsibility, love, creativity, gratification of basic needs, and personal growth. Subjective experience rather than outward behavior receives the primary emphasis. "The humanist is concerned with the individual, the exceptional, the unpredictable rather than seeking to study the regular, the universal, and the conforming." [4] As a counselor, he is person-centered rather than problem-centered. He is concerned with what the counselee as an individual is experiencing at each moment of the counseling dialogue. He avoids interpretations, explanations, and evaluations in order to preserve the personal meaning of the data offered by the counselee.

This emphasis on subjective experience springs from phenomenology, a contemporary school of philosophy. Phenomenology questions *What* is there rather than Why, Whence, or Wherefore. [5] It advocates a direct, immediate, and deliberately naïve approach to experience. [6] It maintains that human actions follow from subjective experience rather than from external, objective reality. Accordingly, each individual is the center of his changing world of experience, and this world has meaning only insofar as it is related to himself.

When phenomenology is applied to counseling, it stresses the need to see the matter from the counselee's point of view, to discover what is existentially real for him, rather than to arrive at a theoretical evaluation of his problem. [7] Obviously the counselor cannot enter the counselee's person and have direct access to his experience. The subject-object split always prevails, but he can arrive at an approximation of the way the counselee looks at the world. He can recognize that his own views, prejudices, and biases influence his response to the counselee. [8] He can be flexible enough to work from the counselee's interpretation of the matter rather than from his own. Those who follow this approach are convinced that this concentration on the counselee's subjective world helps him see the limitations of his particular view of the facts, so that he can clarify his thinking, reach a decision, and act.

In the following chapters we shall consider some of the main concepts of humanistic psychology and apply them to the unique task of the religious counselor. Although the emphasis is on the humanistic approach, the presentation also includes some of the findings of psychoanalysis and learning theory that complement the humanistic position. We have insisted throughout that understanding the subjective experiences of the individual is a requisite of effective counseling.

The Counselee

Counseling involves a dialogue between the counselor and the counselee, a person seeking assistance in a time of need. The position of the counselee is different from that of a patient or client. Usually the person who comes for religious counseling is not a "patient" because he is not sick; he is not a "client" because he is not asking for business or professional information. He expects to find in the religious counselor not a doctor or lawyer but an understanding, open person who can help him come to a better understanding of himself as a *Christian* and to view in light of his Christian commitment the particular set of circumstances in which he finds himself. It may not be necessary for him to receive information or advice at all. Once he has come to this understanding, he can usually take steps to resolve the problem which prompted him to come for help.

Counselees seeks out a clergyman for many reasons. We can mention just a few as examples: marriage conflict, indecision about an impending marriage, an argument with and loss of a friend, trouble with an aged parent or a delinquent son, anxiety about handling death or illness in one's family, financial losses, loss of faith, or failure of religion to have meaning in one's life. The counselee usually does not expect the contact to bring about any radical change in his personality or to make psychological symptoms disappear, as would probably occur in psychiatric treatment and psychological counseling; rather he looks for assistance in coping with what he considers "normal" problems of everyday living. It may well happen, however, that what he thinks of as an ordinary problem is far from ordinary; in this case a referral to a competent professional is in order, since the religious counselor is not equipped to treat mental illness.

Plan of Discussion

The discussion that follows will be divided into three sections: (1) the nature, scope, and aim of counseling in general and of religious counseling in particular; (2) the counselor and his personal qualifications; (3) the counselee and his inner experiences and needs. We shall first consider the assets and limitations of several different approaches to counseling. We shall then discuss religious counseling as a distinct form of dialogue whose effectiveness results from elucidating and deepening the counselee's Christian commitment. Since religious counseling mainly involves talking about religious and moral values, we shall consider the nature of these values and describe their central importance in the counseling process. Second, we shall focus on the counselor, who helps the counselee by giving of himself. The qualities of his personality have much to do with his success or failure. Finally, we shall consider the counselee's inner world, his means of coping with stress, and his affective responses; we shall treat the needs that prompt him to seek help and the ways of meeting these needs; and we shall point out differences between the normal and the abnormal person so that the clergyman can decide which counselees he is equipped to help and which ones he should refer to a psychiatrist or clinical psychologist.

References

[1] R. S. Woodworth and M. R. Sheehan, *Contemporary Schools of Psychology* (New York: The Ronald Press Company, 1964), pp. 10–12.

[2] Frank T. Severin, *Humanistic Viewpoints in Psychology* (New York: McGraw-Hill Book Company, 1965), p. xiv.

3 Joseph W. Krutch, *Human Nature and Human Condition* (New York: Random House, Inc., 1959).

4 James F. T. Bugental, *Challenges of Humanistic Psychology* (New York: McGraw-Hill Book Company, 1967), p. 8.

5 Willis E. Dugan, ed., *Counseling Points of View* (Minneapolis: University of Minnesota Press, 1959), pp. 42–43.

6 Renato Taguiri and Luigi Petrullo, *Person Perception and Interpersonal Behavior* (Stanford, California: Stanford University Press, 1958), p. 34.

7 Theodore Million, *Theories of Psychopathology* (Philadelphia, Pa.: W. B. Saunders, Co., 1967), p. 262.

8 D. H. Ford and H. B. Urban, *Systems of Psychotherapy* (New York: John Wiley & Sons, Inc., 1963), pp. 449–50.

2

Approaches to Counseling

The word *counseling* currently has a variety of meanings, ranging from giving friendly advice to administering psythotherapy. In its popular use, counseling often means simply offering advice. This definition would include any situation in which one individual advises another about a matter of concern to him. Sometimes this kind of advising involves the knowledge of abstract principles. For example, the pastor acts as a counselor when he applies theological principles to the solution of a marriage problem, even though he does not take psychological implications into consideration. In this case he focuses on the problem rather than the individual. If a second individual were to come to him with approximately the same problem, he would no doubt offer the same suggestions. In this book we shall use the term *counseling* in a fuller and more psychological context. The orientation will be toward the individual rather than toward the abstract problem.

Counseling Research

Professional counseling involves a face-to-face relationship in which a trained person tries through verbal and nonverbal communication to help another person develop himself more fully or solve a worrisome problem.[1] Facts and theories furnished by psy-

8

chological research are instrumental in accomplishing this end.[2] The counselor chooses certain of these facts and theories and evolves his own method of counseling. During the past three or four decades, psychology has produced a considerable amount of information on human behavior, some of which has withstood the scrutiny of further research and clinical use to become the basis of counseling practice.

The research psychologist tries to determine what occurs when two people assume the relationship of counselor and counselee.[3] Since this interaction is so complex, it should not surprise us to discover that different research psychologists tend to focus on different aspects and as a result may espouse divergent views of counseling. For example, one may be impressed by the reasoning process that enables the counselor to diagnose the problem accurately and to guide the counselee to a sound solution; another may prefer to emphasize the value of the relationship that develops in the counseling interview. These preferences give rise to two theories of counseling, one that stresses the psychological knowledge and technical skill of the counselor, and another that stresses the psychological phenomenon of acceptance. There is probably much truth in each position, but the view one accepts depends upon one's psychological convictions and past experience. In this way many theories of counseling have been formulated.

Types of Counseling

Current principles of counseling not only derive from a variety of theoretical positions but also apply to many diverse problems.[4] In schools, counseling is used to establish a student's educational goals and to increase his motivation. In this instance, the principles of counseling are intended to help a student select a major area of study, plan his scholastic program, and remove any blocks to progress that he should meet. Vocation counseling is another common type. Often with the help of psychological tests, the vocational counselor helps the counselee choose a profession or occupation that suits his abilities and interests. Much present-day counseling is administered by social workers who assist others in working through family problems. Still another type is personal counseling, which is the proper function of the counseling psychologist. In this instance the emphasis is placed upon aiding normal personality growth and adjustment. Finally, there is the type of counseling done by the pastor or school chaplain, which we shall call religious counseling. Its primary objective is to foster a fuller Christian life; a subsequent objective may be to apply Christian principles to problems in everyday living.

Not infrequently the lines of division among the various types of counseling are obscured.[5] The counseling psychologist may find himself acting as a vocational counselor and vice versa. The same is true of the religious counselor; often the chaplain finds himself undertaking what might well be considered personality counseling. Since man's mental life is not separated into air-tight compartments, this overlapping of functions should be neither surprising nor disturbing.

No matter what the purpose of the counseling may be, the underlying techniques are often quite similar. The vocational counselor dealing with an occupational choice may employ essentially the same principles that the counseling psychologist would apply to a problem of adjustment. Let us consider briefly some of the suppositions basic to most types of counseling.

Basic Suppositions in Counseling

In a technical sense, counseling is not merely giving advice to help an individual adjust to a vexing situation.[6] If it were, anyone with a little common sense could probably be a counselor. It has been established, however, that in many instances giving advice or information has little effect.[7] Man is too complex a being to respond like a computer to the input of pat answers. He may understand the advice, but his emotional attitudes may keep him from accepting and acting on it. Often a person's reason for seeking help has little to do with facts or answers. If he meets with a barrage of "sound" suggestions, he will probably close his ears and look for the nearest exit. Either he is not seeking answers or he is not yet ready to listen to suggestions. He is seeking what the professional would call counseling. Of course, situations may arise in which it is appropriate to give advice or information, but a clear distinction should be maintained between this process, sometimes called guidance, and the process of counseling.

Counseling involves something more than a solution to immediate problems.[8] Its ultimate goal is an inner growth which will equip the individual to face and solve future problems on his own. Counseling aims at bringing about lasting changes as well as immediate decisions and actions. This inner growth is a goal not only of personality counseling but of every type of counseling. Even the vocational counselor, who is faced with the immediate task of helping someone find a suitable occupation, hopes that as a result of counseling the counselee will have a better understanding of his abilities and skills and will be better prepared to make future occupational choices. The religious counselor engaged in counseling in the sense defined above is not satisfied with imparting whatever applied theology has reference to an immediate situation; he hopes that his efforts will bring about a deeper commitment to the Christian way of life.

Some think of counseling as primarily an intellectual process. They think of the good counselor as one who has a knack for "seeing through" situations and getting to "the heart of the matter," as a man of insight who can apply skillfully the rules of logical reasoning and come up with the correct answer. Research has shown, however, that effective counseling is more an emotional than an intellectual process.[9] It is becoming more and more evident that many people can see on an intellectual level, even before they seek counseling, what they must do to remedy a problem; but because of faulty emotional responses they are unable to act. A father may perceive clearly that he should exert firmer control over his delinquent son but at the same time may be unable to do so. Telling him that he needs to be firm is of little help since he already knows or at least suspects this. His problem is rooted in something less evident. He may feel inadequate as a father and consequently may be unable to muster sufficient strength to control his son. Counseling concentrates on the less evident feelings and emotions that affect personality. These emotions often provide the actual motivation for actions which we attribute to reason and judgment.

The Counseling Relationship

Recent writing on the counseling process stresses above all the importance of the relationship that exists between counselor and counselee.[10] Although the process may seem to the counselee to be simply a matter of receiving another person's insight, it actually involves much more. During each interview a constant interplay of feelings, emotions, and ideas results in meaningful communication between the people involved. In the ideal situation the counselor accepts the counselee fully, or in other words takes a positive attitude toward him and regards him as a person of worth and dignity having the right to make his own decisions.[11] The counselor conveys this attitude to the counselee subtly, through his actions. In this way he creates an atmosphere of trust and confidence that allows the counselee to feel relaxed and unthreatened and to talk about things he previously refused to face. This relationship gives the counselee a freedom to look within himself and to solve his problems on his own; eventually he will gain the inner strength he needs to tackle future problems. One of the most baffling things for the counselee to understand is why the thinking he does in the counseling room has more effect than the thinking he does at home by himself. The chief difference between the two situations lies in the relationship that is at the center of any effective counseling.

In addition to creating a nonthreatening atmosphere, the counseling relationship gives the counselee the opportunity to experience a wholesome relationship with another person. He can then profit from this experience and form similar relationships with people he meets in the normal course of his life. These friendships, in turn, will contribute to further personality growth.

In summary, it can be said that current practice, for the most part, looks upon counseling as a process that is (1) more permanent in effect than guidance; (2) broader in purpose than mere problem-solving; (3) concerned with emotions, attitudes, and inner growth; and (4) vitally dependent upon the relationship between the counselor and the counselee. To illustrate these points, let us consider briefly a case presentation.

> Mrs. M. has just been abandoned by her husband after ten years of marriage. From the beginning the marriage has been unstable. She and her husband have had periodic violent arguments, and on several occasions he has stormed out of the house, to return only after three or four days. In a state of considerable distress Mrs. M. goes to her pastor. Outwardly she gives every indication that she is seeking nothing more than advice. Should she make arrangements for the care of the children and then find a job? Should she start divorce pro-

ceedings and demand that the husband support the children? If he comes back, should she take him in just as she has done before? After listening to Mrs. M's account, the pastor focuses attention on the instability of the marriage and its effect on the children. He speaks of an obligation to provide an atmosphere where the children can grow up as good, Christian people. He then suggests some specific arrangements for the support of the children. He advises her to consult a lawyer about the best ways to make her husband contribute to their support. Mrs. M. appears dissatisfied with the advice and offers many rather superficial objections. The pastor tries to convince Mrs. M. that she must face the reality of her situation. The interview ends with both parties showing resentment.

As Mrs. M. becomes even more distraught, a friend recommends that she consult with a priest who has had some specialized training in counseling. The priest immediately recognizes Mrs. M.'s emotional turmoil and concludes that any attempt at making decisions would be useless. He becomes an interested listener. For more than an hour Mrs. M. pours out her hostility and anger toward her husband and indicates that she feels confined as the mother of four small children. The priest encourages the release of feelings and occasionally, by means of well-formulated comments, shows that he understands her feelings. Toward the end of the hour she begins to realize that in some way she is contributing to her marital problem and her emotional condition. She finishes by saying that she feels much better and wants to come back again. Four days later she arrives and announces that her husband has returned. She says that even under the most trying circumstances they have been able to talk with each other; they have discussed their latest argument and have decided that both were at fault. She then asks if the counselor would be willing to see both of them, as they both think they need help if the marriage is to be saved.

In this example we see two approaches to a problem: guidance and counseling. The pastor chose to offer guidance. He made appropriate and reasonable suggestions for solving the immediate family problem. Mrs. M. had a marriage difficulty of long duration. She had never been able to find a satisfactory solution on her own. For these reasons the pastor assumed an authoritarian role and made some definite suggestions toward a solution, like finding means of support for the children and investigating legal action. Behind his thinking was the conviction that Mrs. M. could not act without outside help and that she needed him to guide her into making decisions. He overlooked almost completely the way her emotional attitudes were affecting her. He was more interested in suggesting reasonable solutions than in developing a human relationship. As a result the interview failed to achieve its purpose.

The counselor, on the other hand, immediately evaluated the situation and concluded that it did not call for giving advice. He concentrated on permitting emotional release and forming a working relationship. He won Mrs. M.'s confidence by becoming an *interested* listener. His attentiveness made her realize that he was concerned not just about the abstract marriage problem but about her personally. He listened to her hour-long tirade, even though he may have thought that some of her grievances were petty or unjustified. He never became angry, showed opposition or sided with the husband. For the time being he simply tried to understand what Mrs. M. was saying and experiencing. As a result, Mrs. M. was able to express openly many emotional attitudes that she had long banished from her conscious mind. She could then see what part these attitudes were playing in her marriage difficulty; but more important, she felt that someone understood her and she found this experience so encouraging that she looked forward to returning for another session. Most important, the counseling brought about an inner growth which made her strong enough to face herself and her husband as she has not done before. She was able to reach the conclusion that she needed help as much as her husband.

Approaches to Counseling

Counselors can assume several different attitudes in their work, such as an authoritarian, a counselor-centered, a nondirective, or a counselee-centered approach. First, if a counselor chooses the authoritarian approach, he takes the leading or directing role.[12] He determines what he considers the best solution and attempts to make the counselee accept this choice. For example, a young woman who has recently graduated from high school is undecided about whether she should accept a proposal of marriage or continue her education in order to become a teacher and fulfill a childhood goal. In this case the authoritarian counselor presupposes either that the girl cannot make her own decision or that he, because of his greater experience, can make a better choice. He evaluates her emotions and attitudes and looks for underlying motives. He is not satisfied merely to give superficial advice; once he is convinced of the correct choice, he tries actively to make the counselee accept it.

Although there are situations which call for an authoritarian approach, research and experience show that it is the least effective method. Its value is highly disputed. For one thing, this technique does not encourage inner growth and self-understanding, since it takes most of the initiative away from the counselee and makes him dependent on the counselor. It might be added that some counselors function without realizing it from an authoritarian frame of reference, which they reveal in many of their mannerisms.

A second position is the counselor-centered approach, which emphasizes the role of the counselor.[13] In this case the counselor does not assume an authoritarian role, although he is more concerned with his own knowledge, technical skill, and personal reactions than he is with the inner world of the counselee. He views the counselee's problem either from his own or from an abstract point of reference. He is more interested in the content of the problem than in the person who is seeking help. He relies heavily on his own knowledge of the area in which the problem falls and chooses the best methods for conveying this knowledge to the counselee. He does not completely ignore emotions, attitudes, and the counseling relationship, but these are not uppermost in his mind. The counselor who adopts this method is usually convinced that the counselee cannot solve his problem without considerable help. The counselor's main contribution is a thorough evaluation of the problem and the application of special persuasive techniques. He differs from the authoritarian counselor in his use of indirect methods. He does not force a decision but rather leads and guides. He often controls the interaction between himself and the counselee.

The opposite of an authoritarian approach is a nondirective one; the opposite of a counselor-centered approach is a counselee-centered one. The nondirective approach is most frequently associated with Carl Rogers, who in recent years has preferred to use the term *client-centered*.[14] In this technique, the function of the counselor is to understand the counselee's emotional experiences so well that he "gets under the skin" of the counselee and comprehends the world as he sees it. "He tries to get within and to live the attitudes expressed instead of observing, to catch every nuance of the changing nature; in a word, to absorb himself completely in the attitudes of the other." [15] The counselor does not, however, become so immersed in the counselee's feelings of fear and hate that he experiences similar feelings; rather he tries to perceive these feelings as the counselee experiences them. In this approach the counselor is not just a passive listener who responds with affective responses that are automatic. He is vitally active, trying "to perceive the world of the client as he sees it, to perceive the client himself as he is seen by himself, to lay aside all perceptions from the external frame of reference while doing so, and to communicate something of this empathic understanding to the client." [16] A presupposition of this approach is the conviction that the counselee has the capacity to solve his own problems if he is given the opportunity; he has been unable to do so previously because of the threatening atmosphere in which he lives. The counselor's function is to create an atmosphere that is nonthreatening. In this approach he does not probe or investigate; he does not ask questions; he does not give information or advice; he does not lead the counselee, even indirectly. His main contribution is his attitude of acceptance and willingness to understand. [17] Through this attitude he establishes a positive, nonthreatening relationship with the counselee which gives him strength to solve his own problems.

A final approach is the counselee-centered one. It is quite similar to the nondirective approach in that the emphasis is placed on the counselee, who is encouraged to express his thoughts, attitudes, and feelings. It differs only in that the counselor does not limit his activity merely to entering the counselee's inner world but becomes somewhat directive if the occasion demands it. At times he sees a place for investigating and questioning. He is convinced that there are situations when the counselee needs help in reaching decisions and solving problems. He offers such help, however, only after he is convinced that he perceives and understands as fully as possible the counselee's inner world.

To stimulate free expression, the counselor may make use of open-ended questions. He may sometimes center the discussion on a confused point so that the counselee can begin to see it more clearly.

Probing is kept to a minimum. The counselee is encouraged "to take the ball and run with it." The emphasis is on the counselee's own experiences and not on some abstract problem. The counselor tries to create the impression that he is interested in the counselee and respects him as an individual. In most instances, he gives as little advice as possible and tries to instill the idea that everyone is free to make his own decisions and is responsible for his own actions. When a decision is reached the counselor respects it, just as he respects the person of the counselee.

Up to this point we have described the nature of counseling, the way it differs from guidance or giving advice, and four approaches to it: authoritarian, counselor-centered, nondirective, and counselee-centered. We shall now consider the nature of one type of counseling, religious counseling.

References

[1] H. B. English and A. C. English, *A Comprehensive Dictionary of Psychological and Psychoanalytic Terms* (New York: Longmans, Green & Co., 1958), p. 127.

[2] Dean Johnson, *Marriage Counseling* (Englewood Cliffs, N.J.: Prentice-Hall, Inc., 1961), p. 8.

[3] Frederick C. Thorne, *Principles of Personality Counseling* (Brandon, Vermont: *Journal of Clinical Psychology*, 1950), p. 85.

[4] James F. Adams, *Problems in Counseling* (New York: The Macmillan Company, 1962), p. 1.

[5] Thorne, *op. cit.*, pp. 19–21; Edward S. Bordin, *Psychological Counseling* (New York: Appleton-Century-Crofts, 1955), pp. 17–22.

[6] Milton E. Hahn and Malcolm S. MacLean, *General Clinical Counseling* (New York: McGraw-Hill Book Company, 1950), p. 4.

[7] Leona E. Tyler, *The Work of the Counselor* (New York: Appleton-Century-Crofts, 1953), p. 14.

[8] Lawrence M. Brammer and Everett L. Shostrom, *Therapeutic Psychology* (Englewood Cliffs, N.J.: Prentice-Hall, Inc., 1960), pp. 270–71.

[9] Tyler, *op. cit.*, p. 15.

[10] Tyler, *op. cit.*, p. 15.

[11] Carl R. Rogers, *Client-Centered Therapy* (New York: Houghton Mifflin Company, 1951). R. May, *Man's Search for Himself* (New York: W. W. Norton & Company, Inc., 1953).

[12] J. F. Adams, *op. cit.*, p. 6.

[13] *Ibid.*, p. 7.

[14] *Ibid.*, p. 9.

[15] Rogers, *op. cit.*, p. 29.

[16] Rogers, *op. cit.*, p. 29.

[17] Carl R. Rogers, *On Becoming a Person* (Boston: Houghton Mifflin Company, 1961), p. 50.

3
The Nature
of Religious Counseling

Religious counseling is a type of counseling undertaken by a person who has a strong commitment to and specialized training in religion. This type of counseling is done by a pastor in a parish, a chaplain in a hospital or in the armed services, or a counselor in a school with a religious affiliation. It is sometimes also called pastoral counseling when it refers to the work of clergymen. Though religious counseling can be practiced by members of any faith, for our purposes we shall restrict its definition to any type of counseling practiced by someone trying to help another person find spiritual awareness and live happily and effectively as a Christian.

Religious counseling is not the same as either psychotherapy or the counseling offered by the professional psychologist.[1] Some religious counselors may be trained psychologists, but when they function in this capacity they are not necessarily engaged in the work of the religious counselor. Religious counseling is a special type of communication between two people, one of whom seeks to improve the spiritual welfare of the other. The religious dimension clearly differentiates this type of counseling from the practice of psychiatry, clinical psychology, or social work. If there is some overlap with other types of counseling, it is incidental to the main purpose of the counseling. Religious counseling helps the individual deal with problems in living that involve, either directly or indirectly, his Christian commitment. Religious counseling finds and focuses on the religious dimension that exists in every problem.

Glock and Stark divide the religious dimension into five sub-dimensions: (1) experiential; (2) ritualistic; (3) ideological; (4) intellectual; and (5) consequential.[2] The experiential dimension includes all those feelings, perceptions, and sensations through which an individual communicates in some way with God. The ritualistic dimension encompasses his religious practices, such as his worship, prayer, and participation in the sacraments. The ideological dimension consists of the values and beliefs to which the religious person adheres. The intellectual dimension involving the religious person is knowledge about the basic tenets of his faith. And finally, the consequential dimension embraces man's relation to man as a consequence of his Christian commitment—and the secular effects of his religious belief, practice, and experience. The dialogue in religious counseling most often concerns this latter dimension, but it can easily revolve around any one of the five.

The Changing View of Religious Counseling

Until quite recently, the scope of religious counseling has been somewhat vague and undefined. Any type of communication involving a clergyman as a counselor has been included. The exact nature and purpose of the contact with the counselee have often remained unspecified. The right to function in the capacity of religious counselor has presumably sprung from ordination, theological training, or simply from one's position in a church or school. Clergymen have often completed few, if any, formal courses in psychology and counseling during their seminary years. It was assumed that a broad liberal arts education and technical theological training adequately equipped them for counseling Christians.

During the past decade many seminaries have seen the limitations of this assumption and have added a series of courses in pastoral psychology. To help the clergyman already engaged in the ministry, several universities have conducted special institutes and workshops in pastoral counseling.[3] The result of these undertakings has been a more professional attitude and increased effectiveness. A similar series of workshops has also been conducted for nuns engaged in counseling the members of their own religious communities or the students in their schools.

Three Questions

Before the individual can be fully effective in the role of religious counselor, he needs to ask himself three questions: (1) Who am I as a religious counselor? (2) What do I do as a religious counselor? (3) What is the purpose of my counseling? He then needs to find answers that are personally meaningful and specify adequately his obligations and responsibilities. If he fails to face these issues, he is likely to drift toward psychiatry or clinical psychology, neglecting the important and much-needed office of religious counselor.

The Psychiatrist and the Religious Counselor

In suggesting a possible answer to the first question, "Who am I as a religious counselor?" it might be helpful to begin by pointing out who the religious counselor is not. First of all, he is not a substitute for the psychiatrist. The goals of psychiatry are, for the most part, clearly delineated and they differ from those of religious counseling. The psychiatrist is a person with medical training who has chosen the treatment of the mentally ill as his area of specialization. In addition to the usual four-year course in medical school and internship in a hospital, he usually completes a three-year residency in psychiatry. During this period he learns techniques and methods, including psychotherapy, which are used in treating mental disorders. It is in the practice of this skill that the work of the psychiatrist is sometimes mistakenly thought to be quite similar to that of the pastoral counselor.

Psychotherapy can be defined in several different ways, according to one's theoretical leanings. There are, however, elements common to most of the definitions; perhaps the most important of these is the professional relationship that is established between the therapist and the patient.[4] Wolberg has defined psychotherapy as follows:

> Psychotherapy is the treatment, by psychological means, of problems of an emotional nature in which a trained person deliberately establishes a professional relationship with a patient with the object 1) of removing, modifying, or retarding existing symptoms, 2) of mediating disturbed patterns of behavior, and 3) of promoting positive personality growth and development.[5]

In this definition there are several elements which clearly distinguish the specific aims of psychotherapy from those of religious counseling. First of all, the psychiatrist considers psychotherapy a form of treatment, like shock therapy, drug therapy, and occupational therapy. The priest or minister engaged in counseling does not consider the counselee to be sick and in need of treatment. For the most part, he is dealing with individuals who are able to function within the range of normality.[6] Even though he may deny any sharp distinction between normal and abnormal, the psychiatrist generally treats individuals who manifest deficiencies like repeated attacks of anxiety, irrational fears, inability to form normal social relationships, or depression and suicidal tendencies. The patient seeks psychiatric care in an effort to find some relief from these symptoms. It is true that on occasion these same symptoms may cause an individual to seek pastoral counseling, but in this case the individual either mistakenly thinks that religion is the answer to his psychological difficulties or simply wants a little common-sense advice.

A second characteristic which distinguishes psychotherapy from religious counseling is the type of education that is required. The psychiatrist undergoes intensive training to equip him for treating the mentally ill. He attends many seminars on psychopathology and techniques in therapy. He has many hours of supervised experience in treating neurotic and psychotic patients. In contrast, the education of the priest or minister is much more academic. He is primarily a theologian in both the speculative and practical sense and is often more concerned with content than with methodology. He may have had one or two courses in psychology, but these emphasized understanding human behavior rather than treating it.

The third distinction between the two professions is the goal each is trying to achieve. Colby states: "The goal of psychotherapy is to relieve the patient of distressing neurotic symptoms or discordant personality characteristics which interfere with his satisfactory adaptation to a world of people and events." [7] The principal goal of religious counseling, on the other hand, is to improve the individual's spiritual and moral welfare. The religious counselor does not set out to rid the counselee of neurotic symptoms and bring about personality change, though these things may occasionally result from the counseling. The main efforts of the religious counselor are directed more toward helping the individual lead a Christian life than toward physical or psychological improvement. Sometimes to achieve this end the counselor may have to deal with minor adjustment problems, but he should be careful that he does not take on psychological problems beyond his level of training.

The final element of psychotherapy given in the above definition, the establishment of a professional relationship, does not distinguish psychotherapy sharply from religious counseling. As we have suggested, this relationship is thought to be the most important part of the psychotherapeutic process. It offers the most probable reason why several types of psychotherapy appear to be effective in spite of their different techniques. A person-to-person relationship also plays a major role in religious counseling.[8] Unless the clergyman establishes rapport with the counselee, the counseling will probably have little value. It seems safe to say, however, that the psychiatrist-patient relationship is not the same as the clergyman-counselee relationship, even though the two may have common elements. The similarity between them probably explains why the clergyman is sometimes called the "poor man's psychiatrist." Actually the two professions are distinct and complementary. The clergyman sometimes needs the services of the psychiatrist to prepare the individual psychologically to follow his Christian commitment; the psychiatrist sometimes needs the services of the clergyman to give spiritual meaning to the patient's life.

The Psychologist and
the Religious Counselor

During the past ten years psychotherapy has been practiced not exclusively by psychiatrists, but also by some clinical psychologists and psychiatric social workers. The members of these two professions have become more and more involved in psychotherapy; they usually consider it less as a treatment and more as a psychological process intended to promote personality reorientation and growth.[9] Nevertheless, the general aim of the clinical psychologist and social worker is closer to the psychiatrist than to the religious counselor in that the emphasis is psychological and social rather than religious.

The clinical psychologist is a professional working in a field akin to psychiatry. The academic nature of his education, however, differentiates him from the psychiatrist. Most clinical psychologists have earned a doctoral degree and frequently have completed a year or more of internship in a hospital for the mentally ill. Counseling, psychotherapy, and evaluation of psychological tests are some of the major functions of the clinical psychologist. The psychiatric social worker usually has a master's degree in social work with an emphasis in caring for the mentally ill. Under the direction of a psychiatrist or clinical psychologist, he often handles initial interviews and sometimes counseling and psychotherapy.

There is, however, no definitive distinction between psychotherapy and counseling. Some consider counseling simply a less intensive form of psychotherapy.[10] Others look upon it as a process limited to the problems of normal people.[11] Some say that counseling primarily deals with the conscious mind and psychotherapy with the unconscious.[12] The present trend in counseling psychology is to concentrate more on the person and less on the problem; the emphasis, however, is on the person's psychological reactions rather than on his religious experiences.[13] It is this emphasis that, despite their shared concerns, differentiates the psychological counselor from the religious counselor. Both may concentrate on the person, but one is primarily concerned with his mental and emotional well-being, whereas the other is concerned with his spiritual and moral well-being.

Who Is the Religious Counselor?

Who, then, is the religious counselor? First of all he has the sense of personal identity that each of us develops in the process of becoming a mature adult.[14] Through self-observation, experience, and reflection, we come to recognize ourselves as distinct individuals. We learn that our own ways of thinking, feeling, and acting differ in many respects from the reactions of others. We become aware of ourselves as people who relate to other people and objects in our own peculiar manner. The individual who has developed this sense of identity knows who he is and does not try to be someone he is not. He does not take his identity from a membership in a group. He recognizes that he is a distinct individual with certain assets and limitations.

As we mature, we develop a self-awareness which lets us know whether we are acting like ourselves or unlike ourselves. We form an approximate idea of the way we usually think, feel, and act. These reactions become criteria by which we judge whether the real self is operating or some representation of what we would like to be or think we should be.

The religious counselor must have developed this sense of personal identity. If he hopes to succeed, he must be himself and cannot merely play the role of counselor. He must know who he is and be unafraid to reveal himself to the counselee. Self-understanding is an essential quality for any type of counselor or psychotherapist. The counselor who is confused and doubtful about his own personal identity cannot help another in his search for identity. Since one function of religious counseling is to help the counselee find his identity as a Christian, the counselor must have a clear sense of his own identity as a Christian. He must be a mature Christian. The mature Christian is one who has taken the message of the Gospel and made it an integral part of himself. His actions flow spontaneously from his Christian belief and values. He follows in the footsteps of Jesus Christ because he is convinced that He is "the way, the truth, and the life."

The Clergyman-Counselor

The religious counselor may be, secondly, a priest or minister. Whenever he functions as a counselor he takes his office with him. Being a clergyman involves a specific type of training, ordination, and experience which make an impact upon the personality of the clergyman and change the way he thinks, feels, and acts. These factors make him a different person from the secular counselor who works in the area of counseling psychology, but who has not had seminary training, the experience of ordination, or the subsequent experiences that are a normal part of the clergyman's life, such as administering the sacraments and preparing the dying to meet God. In addition to possessing special graces that accompany sacred ordination, the clergyman-counselor should be committed more intensely than the layman to Christian values. These values should be internalized and made a part of his personality. They manifest themselves in the counseling session indirectly if not overtly. It is precisely this commitment or dedication to Christianity that brings the counselee to the clergyman or "God-centered" counselor rather than to the secular counselor.

Obligations and Responsibilities

Finally, the religious counselor is just as much a counselor as any other individual engaged in the various fields of counseling. He therefore has all the obligations and responsibilities of a secular counselor. As we have said, a counselor is a person who intentionally establishes a professional relationship to achieve a specific goal.[15] To a certain extent he takes the life and welfare of the counselee into his own hands. Frequently the way the counselee will subsequently live hinges to some degree upon what takes place during the counseling sessions. In religious counseling the counselee's spiritual welfare is of primary concern, but it not infrequently happens that his method of adjusting to life in general is also changed.

If the religious counselor has been ordained, he can draw on many special sources of strength, the most important of which is the grace of ordination. He is never simply a counselor; God works through him as a "called" person. The sacrament of ordination makes him a medium through which God speaks to the souls of others. In addition to this grace, the clergyman-counselor's (as well as any other religious counselor's) relationship with God, especially in the Person of Jesus Christ, influences the outcome of his counseling. A true devotion to God cannot help but be reflected during each session. It becomes an incentive to the counselee to open himself to the workings of divine grace. The clergyman-counselor also draws from years of seminary education. He is a trained theologian versed in the ways that God relates to the world. His training has been practical as well as speculative. During the past few years there has been an added emphasis on the pastoral aspect of theology. Possessing knowledge does not necessarily give one the ability of imparting this knowledge to others. This stress on pastoral theology can contribute to better counseling, since it directs attention toward methods of reaching people's minds and feelings. Finally, the religious counselor draws from his past experience. In the long run experience is probably the most essential element in learning the art of counseling. Often the individual counselor develops by trial and error the approaches that are most effective for him. Technical training can offer guidelines, but only experience will demonstrate what the individual can accomplish and what he cannot.

Pitfalls for the Young Counselor

The young priest or minister fresh from the seminary and eager to help people often finds himself in a quandary. He has left the tranquil order of seminary life and finds himself engulfed in the turbulence of a city or suburban parish. He is expected to assume many responsibilities and to fulfill them with some success. He is anxious to serve and perhaps takes on more than he should, involving himself in a type of counseling for which he has neither the time, energy, nor professional competence. He fails to set proper limits on the intensiveness and extent of his counseling. He soon finds that the situation has gone out of control, but he is so deeply involved with his counselees that he does not see how he can terminate these contacts. His effectiveness suffers because he is overwhelmed by the number of people seeking his help.

Success is important to most young counselors. They are overly sensitive about whether or not they are helping other people. They want to make the counselee feel better and leave the office saying: "Thank you so much; you have helped me a great deal." To achieve this response, they may offer some "desperation" advice which may be supportive for the moment but does not help in the long run. Although they are often not aware of it, they can be more concerned with evoking signs or indications of success than with actually helping the counselee. They are concerned about whether the individual will return, and they feel frustrated if he does not. Much of this trouble is rooted in a lack of self-confidence. The young counselor has yet to build an adequate image of himself as a counselor; he needs a number of successes before he is satisfied that he can function well in this role. When he does achieve self-confidence, he will realize that much of what takes place in counseling frequently goes unnoticed by both the counselor and the counselee. The purpose of the counseling is to help the counselee become a better Christian, not to give him false reassurance or make him like the counselor better. Sometimes the price that both the counselor and the counselee must pay is pain and distress, but this result does not mean that the counseling has been ineffective.

What Does
the Religious Counselor Do?

The second question which the religious counselor must ask is "What do I do as a religious counselor?" As we have already seen, the word *counseling* has many possible meanings. This is also true of religious counseling. For some people, religious counseling means giving information and advice. They would say that the clergyman is in much the same position as the lawyer who counsels his client. When the lawyer acts as a professional, he listens to the problem of the client, draws from his knowledge of the law, and then advises the client about how he should conduct his personal or business affairs. People who accept this definition would limit religious counseling to approximately the same function and would say that the clergyman draws from his knowledge of speculative and practical theology and then advises the counselee about how he should conduct himself. We prefer to look on religious counseling as something more than giving advice on the basis of theological principles; there are times when the clergyman engages in counseling but gives no advice and offers no information.

For other people, religious counseling means making suggestions based on personal experience and common sense. Because the counselor is usually regarded as a wise, educated, trustworthy person, his opinions and views are valued. An individual who is perplexed about what he should do in a certain situation comes to the rectory to seek advice from his pastor, a person whom he re-

pects and trusts. He relates his predicament and listens to a response based on the pastor's experiences in dealing with himself
and with other people. Although this is a legitimate type of counseling, once again we prefer to espouse a broader definition of the
term.

Sometimes a man or woman comes to the counselor "just to
talk over something." He does not seek religious instruction or
theological information. He is not looking for an answer to a question and does not want advice about how he should act toward his
wife or child. He simply wants the opportunity to communicate
with someone who he knows is trustworthy and understanding. He
expects the counselor to listen attentively and to show a certain
warmth and acceptance, but he wants "to carry the ball" himself.
He needs someone to give him support and act as a sounding board,
but he wants to make his own decisions. When the counselor fulfills
this need, he is counseling in the psychologist's sense of the term.
Although he may not realize it at the time, he may be rendering a
greater service than he would by suggesting what he considers the
wisest advice. He is giving himself as one human being to another
at a time when this other person has a great need to feel that he is
not alone.

The religious counselor uses the same initial approach as any
other professional counselor, indicating to the counselee that he
understands and accepts him. It is especially important to establish
rapport in the beginning phase of counseling. The religious counselor goes beyond this demonstration of acceptance and understanding, however, to encourage the counselee in his pursuit of a
Christian life. The counselor does this by clarifying and solidifying
tenets of belief, by helping the counselee see for himself solutions
based on Christian teachings, and by assisting him to become more
aware of the divine presence in his everyday life. He persuades the
counselee to "(1) place himself before Christ and the Father, according to the Gospel; (2) accept himself; (3) recognize his real
sin in the sight of Christ; (4) find in Penance—whether received or
given—the sacrament of reconciliation and a proclamation of mercy;
and (5) face his trials in the light of the mystery of the Cross." [16]

At times these ends can be realized through a client-centered
approach, particularly when the counselee is a committed Christian
looking for someone with whom he can discuss his religious ex-

periences and convictions. Conversation helps him to clarify his thoughts and feelings so that he can arrive at decisions based on well-founded Christian principles. When a person discusses a topic with another, he is forced to be logical and orderly. If he simply sits in solitude and tries to think through a problem, he often finds that his mind wanders in all directions and that he seems to be going nowhere. One confused image or idea after another passes through the mind, accompanied by much feeling and emotion but little real thought. Perhaps after hours of worrying and fretting he will have made little progress toward understanding or resolution.

This confusion may be alleviated by attempting seriously to transmit our thoughts to another in conversation. In the first place, we are forced to put all we have to say in sentences. If we offered someone a meaningless stream of unrelated ideas and imaginings, he would not understand what we were talking about, and he would quickly lose interest and stop listening. In addition to speaking in sentences, we must also indicate some connection between our thoughts. The act of formulating our thoughts for conversation often makes them become intelligible. A man may be much more reasonable when he is trying to explain his problem to another then when he works it out on his own. The client-centered approach is often successful because it allows the individual to talk about the impact of spiritual values on his life and through this conversation to discern whether he is truly following the promptings of the Spirit or is merely deceiving himself.

A More Direct Approach

People who come to the religious counselor often lack a full commitment to Christianity. They may be indifferent, lukewarm, or limited in their understanding of Christianity, or they may doubt certain tenets of their faith. In this situation a more direct, instructive approach is needed. No one can commit himself fully to any belief unless he understands its fundamental teachings. If a person consults a religious rather than a secular counselor, he is probably looking for the religious dimension of his problem, but he may not have sufficient knowledge to find it. He may regard his inability to see eye-to-eye with his wife on many major issues merely as a marriage conflict that has little to do with religion. The problem can be approached on two levels, however, the psychological and the religious, and both must be dealt with. The counselor may have to focus on the religious dimension in a direct, forthright manner. In general the counselee does not simply grow into Christianity but must learn what it means to be a Christian; sometimes such learning calls for direct teaching and instruction.

To exemplify this directive approach in religious counseling, let us consider a case.

Miss A., a forty-five-year-old bookkeeper, comes to her pastor after taking an overdose of sleeping pills. In an interview with a psychiatrist at the receiving ward, she mentioned being a member of a Church and was urged to visit her pastor. During the three days of hospitalization she refused to talk about anything of a personal nature. Although this was her second unsuccessful attempt, she insisted strongly that she had never intended to commit suicide and that it was all "a mistake" on her part.

The pastor finds her a pleasant, talkative person, but he feels that her affability is a "smoke-screen." He notes that she avoids talking about what prompted her to take the sleeping pills. She concentrates on superficial worries: financial straits resulting from a poor investment and friction between herself and a sister. After allowing her ample opportunity to vent her feelings about these situations, he begins to turn the interview toward the purpose of life. He moves gradually to the place of religion in one's life, at first keeping his approach general and abstract and then centering on what the counselee sees as the purpose of her life. She admits that religion has always meant a great deal to her. Her firm belief in a personal but demanding God becomes evident. She speaks of finding herself frequently immersed in prayer. She has never doubted God's existence or goodness, even in her most depressed moments, but she thinks He has no use for her. At times she feels that He hates her and has abandoned her. It was during two of these periods that she attempted suicide. She says that at these times she was convinced that she would eventually be condemned to eternal damnation and so wondered why she should suffer all the present torment. She thought it would be better to get it over with once and for all. It is at this point that she brings up spontaneously her unmarried state. She feels that the real purpose of every woman is to bear children.

Since she has failed in this regard, she thinks that God must hate her. She blames herself for not capitalizing on a couple of opportunities to marry, but now that is "water under the bridge" and there is nothing she can do about it. Her whole life has been a failure. She has failed God and herself. The pastor, after reacting to her feelings of depression and hope-lessness, returns to the theme of the meaning of life. He begins to talk about Christian meaning in life, pointing out the differ-ence between her view and that of Christianity. After con-siderable discussion the counselee gradually begins to see that her view is distorted and that there are other life-goals open to the Christian woman; as a result she experiences a greater sense of her own worth. He then turns the interview to the subject of her relationship with God and emphasizes the hope inherent in her ability to experience frequently the divine presence operating in her everyday life.

In this interview the counselor not only promoted an atmo-sphere that would lead to greater self-understanding, but also used positive measures that would make the counselee face religious issues. The counselor's primary concern was to give the counselee a better outlook on life and to bring about religious growth. If the counseling had continued over a number of sessions, the counselor might have found that in the later stages of the process a less directive approach would be more effective.

What is the Purpose of Religious Counseling?

The final question which the religious counselor must ask himself is "What is the purpose of my counseling?" One approach to this question is to compare in terms of scope three types of counseling: religious counseling, psychological counseling, and psychotherapy (Figure 1.) First of all, religious counseling is differ-ent from the other two in that it is concerned with the growth and development of the *Christian*. It is directed toward encouraging the normal person to develop his spiritual capacities rather than toward overcoming serious psychological problems. Abraham Mas-low speaks of two general classifications of human needs: growth-needs and deficiency-needs.[17] By deficiency-needs he means those basic psychological needs that we must fulfill if we are to lead

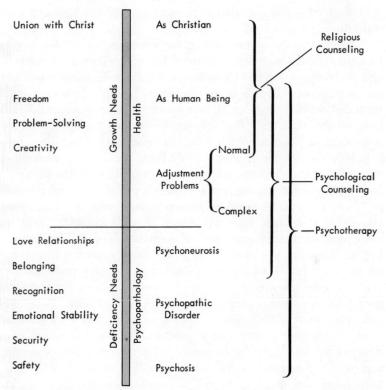

Figure 1. The Scope of Religious Counseling, Psychological Counseling, and Psychotherapy.

normal healthy lives; growth-needs refer to our need for developing the higher human capacities. When the basic psychological needs are not satisfied at least minimally, the person usually manifests some form of psychopathology or psychological illness, such as neurosis, psychopathic disorder, or psychosis.

These deficiency-needs are numerous and complex. To name a few examples, we can include the need to feel safe and secure both physically and psychologically; to feel free from the constant threat of physical harm or death; and to feel competent to withstand the normal pressures of everyday living. We also need to experience appreciation and love from others, both for what we are and for what we do. The fulfillment of these and other basic needs provides the foundation for our psychological health, which is necessary for the growth and development of our higher human capacities.

Before an individual can make effective use of his higher faculties, these lesser demands must be met.[18] To reason logically and precisely, to arrive at conclusive decisions, to think creatively, one must have a degree of psychological health which cannot be sustained when numerous deficiency-needs have gone unfulfilled. One of the main purposes of psychotherapy and psychological counseling—a purpose which religious counseling does not share—is to help the patient or client satisfy these needs either directly or indirectly so that he can function as a relatively effective person.

Besides encouraging people to develop their spiritual faculties as Christians and to grow as human beings, religious counseling also helps them face and resolve, in accordance with Christian principles, the normal problems of everyday living.[19] The psychological counselor also deals with problems of everyday living, but for the most part his practice is limited to complex problems like marriage conflicts with psychological causes or social inadequacies springing from self-rejection. The religious counselor directs his particular point of view even to problems as mundane as financial need. Godin states that every painful situation has a religious dimension.[20] He urges the counselor to be aware of this dimension and to help the counselee become aware of it, even when the relationship of the problem to religion and morality is not readily apparent. This awareness differentiates the work of the religious counselor from that of the psychological counselor.

Openness to God

In considering the purpose of religious counseling we need to look to theology even more than to psychology. Theology treats of the various ways that God has chosen to speak to man. Since listening to God is a vital element in our religious development, one aim of religious counseling is to make the counselee open to His voice. God speaks to an individual through the revealed word as manifested in the Old and New Testaments. He also speaks through the Church and its ministers. He speaks through others and through the seemingly ordinary events of life. Finally, He speaks directly to the individual. The mature Christian is one who can listen to the voice of God as it comes to him from these sources. Sometimes a person reads the scriptures but gains little or no religious insight from them. He regards them as just another piece of literary prose. Although he has been exposed to the word of God, he does not hear it. Another person hears the teaching of the Church through its priests or ministers, but what he hears fails to have any personal meaning for him. Still another person is oblivious of God speaking to him through a husband or wife, a friend, or even an enemy. The message goes unheeded because the individual does not recognize that it comes from God. And finally, the Spirit can speak directly to an individual, urging him to think and act in a certain way, but the inspiration is lost on him. He is too distracted by his inner turmoil to listen to anything else. Religious counseling prepares the individual to listen to God when He speaks.

This view of religious counseling plays down active intervention on the part of the counselor and stresses the action of God in producing spiritual maturity. The main function of the religious counselor is to prepare the way for the Spirit. As St. Paul put it, "I planted, Apollos watered, but God has given the growth" (1 Corinthians, 3, 6). The religious counselor tries to help the counselee regain peace of mind so that the Spirit can work in the soul as It sees fit. The counselor does not take the individual by the hand and lead him to God; on the basis of revelation, it is assumed that if the individual is properly disposed God will draw him to Himself.

Three Obstacles

There are three obstacles that keep people from listening to God: rejection of the Spirit, sin, and emotional turmoil. The first obstacle is found in those who have been exposed to Christianity and offered the gift of faith, but either have refused to accept it or, once having accepted it, have later rejected it. Because of pride and excessive self-love, they have turned a deaf ear to the Spirit. In this case the purpose of counseling is to make the counselee realize why he has rejected this gift.

The second obstacle, sin, is found in those who retain their belief in God but choose their own will in preference to His. They turn their backs on God and as a consequence frequently do not hear the Spirit when it speaks to them. Repeated sin weakens faith so that it gradually becomes less and less meaningful. One goal of religious counseling is to bring about repentence, confession, and reparation, which turn the sinner away from sin and make him once again open to God.

The third obstacle, emotional disturbance, affects those whose inner conflict and frustration are so intense that they no longer possess peace of mind. Fear, anxiety, hostility, and guilt demand most of their attention. There is such an uproar within that the voice of God cannot penetrate their awareness. In this case, if the individual is not seriously disturbed, the religious counselor may help the counselee regain his peace of mind; in a more pathological case, the counselee may have to visit a professional psychotherapist. Once peace has been reestablished the counselor steps aside, allowing God full freedom to work. Spiritual counseling should be more concerned with promoting an awareness of God and His workings than with exhortation and correction. The person who is open to God needs little directive guidance; he needs instead the opportunity to recognize more fully the working of God within himself.

Openness to Self

Openness to God depends upon openness to self. We use self-awareness as a stepping-stone to awareness of God. The person who surrounds himself with protective devices cannot see God working within himself. Self-understanding and self-acceptance are requisites for receiving the Word. This is why religious counseling is often most effective when it follows a client-centered approach and helps the individual face and accept himself as he actually exists. The resultant openness to self prepares the ground for an awareness of the Spirit "who breathes where He will."

Baute says that "pastoral counseling can be described as an interpersonal relationship of acceptance, understanding, and communication between priest (or a clergyman) and a parishioner for the purpose of assisting that person in making choices and decisions, and thus pursue his own Christian vocation according to his capacities with more happiness." [21] Openness to the voice of the Spirit implies not a loss of freedom but increased freedom. The purpose of counseling is to create within the individual freedom to make his decisions on the basis of his own convictions, as these are informed by the Spirit, and not on the basis of compulsion, fear, guilt, or hostility. The acceptance, understanding, and communicativeness of the counselor permit the counselee to realize the freedom he needs to listen to the Spirit. The counselor works at establishing an atmosphere as free as possible from fear and anxiety, one which allows the counselee to look at himself as he actually is and to experience peace and tranquility.

St. Paul in his letter to the Galatians describes how one can determine whether an individual is acting freely according to the promptings of the Spirit: "But the fruit of the Spirit is love, joy, peace, patience, kindness, goodness, faithfulness, gentleness, and self-control" (Galatians 5, 22). Spiritual writers have dealt at length with the discernment of spirits. Among the many signs that God is actually moving an individual are a sincere, continuing desire to imitate Christ, truthfulness and honesty, openness to counsel, flexibility of will, serenity, and humility.[22] The counselee who manifests these qualities should not doubt that he is following the inspiration of the Spirit.

We have suggested answers to three questions: (1) Who am I as a religious counselor? (2) What do I do as a religious counselor? and (3) What is the purpose of my counseling? The answers were based primarily on a counselee-centered approach, whose goal is to open the individual to the voice of God, the Divine Counselor, speaking through the revealed Word, through the Church, through others, and finally directly to each counselee. Religious counseling tries to eliminate the obstacles that keep the individual from listening to the divine promptings.

References

[1] V. V. Herr, S.J., W. J. Devlin, S.J., and F. J. Kobler, *Religion and Mental Health: A Catholic Viewpoint* (New York: Academy of Religion and Mental Health, 1960).

[2] Charles Y. Glock and Rodney Stark, *Religion and Society in Tension* (Chicago: Rand McNally & Co., 1965), pp. 19–21.

[3] William C. Bier, ed., *Problems in Addition* (New York: Fordham University Press, 1962) and *Personality and Sexual Problems in Pastoral Psychology* (New York: Fordham University Press, 1964).

[4] F. E. Fiedler, "A Comparison of Therapeutic Relationships in Psychoanalytic, Non-Directive and Adlerian Therapy," *Journal of Consulting Psychology*, XIV (1950), 436–45.

38 THE NATURE OF RELIGIOUS COUNSELING

```

5 Lewis R. Wolberg, M.D., *The Technique of Psychotherapy*, Part I (New York: Grune & Stratton, Inc., 1967), p. 3. Quoted by permission of Grune & Stratton, Inc.

6 Paschal Baute, "The Work of the Pastoral Counselor," *Insight*, 11, No. 2. (1963), 5.

7 Kenneth M. Colby, M.D., *A Primer for Psychotherapists* (New York: The Ronald Press Company, 1951), p. 3.

8 Baute, *op. cit.*, p. 6.

9 Julian B. Rotter, *Clinical Psychology* (Englewood Cliffs, N.J.: Prentice-Hall, Inc., 1964), pp. 2–9.

10 Leona E. Tyler, *The Work of the Counselor* (New York: Appleton-Century-Crofts, 1953), pp. 193–227.

11 F. C. Thorne, *Principles of Personality Counseling* (Brandon, Vermont: *Journal of Clinical Psychology*, 1950), pp. 301–2.

12 Brammer and Shostram, *op. cit.*, p. 7.

13 Arthur W. Combs and Daniel W. Soper, "The Perceptual Organization of Effective Counselors," *Journal of Counseling Psychology*, X, No. 3 (1963), 222–26.

14 Sidney M. Jourard, *Personal Adjustment* (New York: The Macmillan Company, 1963), pp. 171–73.

15 Dugold S. Arbuckle, *Counseling: An Introduction* (Boston: Allyn & Bacon, Inc., 1964), pp. 133–39.

16 C. Bouchaud, "The Spiritual Director of a Subject in Psychotherapy," *Insight*, VI, No. 3 (1968), 41.

17 Abraham H. Maslow, *Toward a Psychology of Being* (Princeton, N.J.: D. Van Nostrand Co., Inc., 1962), pp. 19–41.

18 Abraham H. Maslow, *Motivation and Personality* (New York: Harper & Row, Publishers, 1954).

19 Seward Hiltner, *Pastoral Counseling* (New York: Abingdon Press, 1959), p. 19.

20 André Godin, S.J., "Transference in Pastoral Counseling," *Theology Digest*, IX (1961), 78–83.

21 Baute, *op. cit.*, p. 6.

22 Antonio Royo, O.P., and Jordan Aumann, O.P., *The Theology of Christian Perfection* (Dubuque, Iowa: Priory Press, 1962), pp. 626–30.
```

4

Values in
Religious Counseling

All the schools of counseling and psychotherapy agree about the essential elements and processes of communication. They differ, however, in the selection and emphasis of topics during the counseling hour.[1] For example, the psychoanalyst tends to focus on material related to the unconscious, whereas the client-centered counselor frequently shows a greater interest in material related to the self-concept and feelings. In religious counseling, the emphasis is placed on values.

Values influence our behavior at almost every moment. We value some things because they keep us alive; others, because they make life more enjoyable; still others, because they give meaning to our lives. Values can be negative as well as positive, causing us to avoid things as well as to desire them.[2] The values of particular concern in the present context are religious and moral ones, those which are included in the value system of Christianity. An example of an essential value in this system is the biblical statement "Love your neighbor as yourself," which implies that the Christian should honor the dignity of the human being and recognize the worth of every man or woman regardless of race or nationality.

39

Learning and Values

Values are the product of identification, education, and personal evaluation.[3] Most children imitate the values of their parents and of other people whom they look upon as important. The development of values follows a pattern somewhat like the pattern of intellectual, emotional, and social development. The young child accepts on faith his parents' value orientations and gives little thought to the "why's" and "wherefore's." In adolescence he begins to seek reasons for the values he has assumed through identification and education.[4] He may pass through a stage when he rejects temporarily or permanently some values which he had not previously called into question. He may even cast aside most of his childhood values and look for new ones. He is undergoing a transition from a childhood to an adult value system. This transition implies a personalization of traditional values previously held only through the influence of parents and teachers. A function of counseling, especially with individuals in these age-groups, is to encourage the maturation of the value system; this can best be achieved if the young person is allowed to work out for himself a personally meaningful philosophy of life.

In adulthood the growth of one's value system does not cease. Most people go through a constant process of reevaluation, reassessing old values, rejecting or modifying some of them, and adopting new ones with the changing times. One would hope that in adult life much of this reevaluation is the outcome of reasoned consideration; often, however, it comes from an admiration for a particular person or group of people. Religious counseling gives the counselee the opportunity to discuss his values freely, consider their advantages and disadvantages, weigh the merits and limitations of new values, and in this way develop a fuller, more meaningful Christian way of living. Religious counseling is an educational process through which an individual can deepen his understanding of Christian values or even accept new ones. It is precisely in this function that the religious counselor differs from other counselors, most of whom maintain that new values should be taught not in the counseling session but in the home, school, and church. The religious counselor often chooses to present both traditional values and ones emerging from renewal within the Church. He does not propagandize or proselytize but simply explains honestly and objectively the beliefs and teachings of the Church as they relate to the contemporary world, allowing the counselee through participation in the dialogue to mull over the significance of these values. The religious counselor sees no incompatibility between the introduction of new values in this way and the procedures followed by most personality counselors. He may even go further and suggest that each counseling system appears to inculcate its own values, as exemplified by remarks from patients who have completed psychoanalysis or client-centered therapy.[5] These expressions indicate the acceptance of new values and a new way of life, and they reflect the particular kind of therapy the patient has undergone.

The religious counselor realizes as a convinced Christian that values originate not just in personal satisfaction or self-actualization but also in some objective order outside of one's being. Religious and moral values are the product of revealed truth, traditional Church teaching, and the work of theologians. If one has not had the opportunity to learn this body of values and integrate it fully into his personality during youth, then he must find some other way to do so—and religious counseling affords just such an opportunity.

The Values of the Counselee

Leona Tyler, an outstanding authority on counseling, believes that values are essential to the counseling process and that all counseling is fundamentally value counseling.[6] She considers that values are intimately connected with impulses, needs, choices, and behavior. Like many others, she asserts that the psychological counselor does not produce new values directly in the counselee, but that he most certainly helps him to look at existing values and to express in words what he sees.[7] He helps the counselee see that his values are numerous and complexly related, that they are sometimes in conflict with one another, and that maladjusted behavior can result from conflicting values. In the climate of a good counseling relationship, the counselee can recognize and face value conflicts more fully than he has previously. In addition, Dr. Tyler maintains that through the process of identification the counselee may adopt some of the counselor's values.

Since Dr. Tyler's procedures in dealing with values are applicable to religious counseling, it will be helpful to relate them in detail.

If we wish to maximize the process of developmental change in values, how shall we handle the counseling situation? Are there any special techniques worth trying? I can only speak about what I have found myself doing. I have found that it is possible to think of the whole counseling process, whether it consists of one interview or twenty, as divided into three stages merging into one another. During the first stage I attempt to create a situation and a human relationship that will encourage the freest possible expression of everything the client feels moved to talk about. My task here is to listen with intense concentration—to try to understand what he is expressing. What I actually say during this first stage is not very important except as it facilitates or hinders the communication between us. Reflection of feeling, general open-ended questions, or questions indicating what I have not understood what he has been saying all seem appropriate. I try to listen especially for the expression of values, what the person wants and prizes, what he condemns and repudiates, what he admires and looks up to. Somewhere in this process I begin to get a glimpse of a sort of design—blurred and confused though it may be—this person's picture of what would constitute a good life for him. It is important not to be in too much of a hurry about this. The counselor's first picture of a client's value structure is likely to be seriously distorted, simply because everything cannot be said at once, and what comes out first may not be most significant. As this structure emerges, I shift my contributions to the interview over toward what might be called interpretation. Clarification is the goal at this second stage. I try to help the person see how different values are related to one another in his experience, how they conflict or alternate, at what point they are confused. This process of interpretation of values does not seem to generate the resistance that often follows other kinds of interpretations, perhaps because of the respect for the integrity of a person we must show if we really take his values seriously. The client and the counselor participate together in this attempt to clarify values and bring them into a coherent order.

In the third stage, I let myself become a reinforcer for the kinds of behavior to which the dominant constructive values lead. As indicated above, I think that counselors cannot avoid having some influence on the values and behavior of their clients whatever they do. We might as well be aware of this influence and exercise some control over it.[8]

Religious counseling sometimes demands an even more direct confrontation with issues involving values. In a number of instances, the individual seeks out the religious counselor precisely because he is bothered by an inability to live up to his values or to resolve the conflicting demands of two opposite, or seemingly opposite, values. An example might be a man who has high ideals but finds it difficult to follow them in the competitive world of business, or a woman who is convinced of the indissolubility of marriage but is faced with marital discord and the possibility of divorce. If the counselor ascertains that both these individuals possess at least average mental health, then he recognizes that these problems center on value issues. Their solution will depend upon a clarification and assessment of conflicting values and obligations. Attempting to deal with these problems on any other basis would be simply skirting the problem and refusing to acknowledge its true nature.

Once the religious counselor has established a working relationship and has gained some insight into the counselee's frame of reference, he is in a position to deal with value issues. In some cases he may be called on to impart information. The counselee wants to determine what the Church teaches in regard to a particular action. His question is frequently a genuine one and not simply an indirect approach to a more basic problem. The counselee is actually seeking answers; to give him evasions results in frustration and disgust. He wants a presentation of theological views and the official position of the Church. For instance, a mother whose seventeen-year-old daughter wants to marry an atheist comes to her pastor seeking the Church's view on such unions. If the pastor decides to use the opportunity to increase the woman's self-understanding rather than to answer her question, he is quite likely to meet with opposition. The mother may want to use the counseling situation as a means of clarifying her own thinking, but she is also seeking the opinion of an authority. The counselor's function is to supply the desired information and to create a relationship which will allow the mother to decide for herself how she should handle the daughter's request. The counselor furnishes the facts and perhaps offers suggestions, but the ultimate decision should come from the counselee.

Often the counselee is not seeking information at all, but is merely uncertain or confused about his values. He is looking for a chance to discuss them with another person. Counselors are often amazed at how readily some people can resolve value conflicts, once they find themselves in an atmosphere of understanding. Others, however, need to be made aware of the way values influence their present thinking and behavior; still others need to have someone point out how one value conflicts with another and produces mental turmoil.

Approaches to Value Counseling

After the initial relationship has been established through the counselor's attentiveness and genuine interest, values usually begin to play a prominent role in the dialogue. One value may be in conflict with another, as in the example of the young physician who finds his practice limiting the time that he should spend with his family. He wants to be a successful physician and feels that he must fulfill his responsibility to his patients; at the same time, he loves his wife and children, wants to spend his evenings and weekends with them, and support them in a manner becoming his profession. Or the conflict may be between one's values and ones basic needs, as in the case of a boy and girl who say that they see the value of not engaging in premarital sexual activity but somehow find themselves necking and petting just about every time they are alone together.

Once the dialogue begins to center around a specific value conflict, the counselor should help the counselee become more aware of the part this conflict plays in his everyday actions. An individual rarely sees a basic human problem as it actually is nor does he realize the degree to which values control, dominate, and determine his life. It is the counselor's task not to make the counselee's experiences more pleasant but to make them more real, so that he can come to terms with the world as it actually is. Both the pleasant and the unpleasant are part of the meaning in one's life.

Focusing on Value Conflicts

Let us consider several techniques that a counselor might use to bring about a fuller realization and acceptance of reality. The first is the technique of focusing on the values that provide the central, recurring theme of the dialogue.[9]

> Mrs. B., the married mother of four small children, comes to the rectory with a baby in her arms. She says that the present state of her marriage has caused her to seek the help of the pastor. She complains about her husband's many faults, none of which provoke much show of feeling. She talks of a constant struggle against poverty. She mentions repeatedly how difficult it is to care for four small children but always shies away from this theme once it has been introduced.

At this point the counselor should focus the dialogue on the matter which seems to concern her most, her attitude toward having children.

> *Mrs. B.:* You don't know how hard it is to take care of two babies who are still in diapers and demand constant attention. I feel exhausted most of the time. I don't even like shopping any more and besides my husband hasn't bought me a new dress in a year. I have to wear these worn out things or take my sister's hand-me-downs.
>
> *Pastor:* You seem to be overwhelmed by all the work that is required to care for your children.
>
> *Mrs. B.:* That is an understatement. I often wonder how I will ever manage to carry on, but my mother is a long-suffering person too. She took an awful lot from my father. I really admire my mother. She is a wonderful person.
>
> *Pastor:* You are worried about what the future has in store. You are not sure you will be able to keep going. Four children are just too many. I wonder what you think the future holds for you?
>
> *Mrs. B.:* Pretty much the same. I guess that I don't see any let up in sight.
>
> *Pastor:* Perhaps another baby and then another after that.
>
> *Mrs. B.:* That's what really bothers me. I don't want any more children and yet I do. I think that we should want all the children God gives us but I don't know how I can ever take care of them.

In this dialogue the pastor persistently returned to what appeared after considerable listening to be the central theme, even though the counselee with equal persistence tried to turn the discussion to less disturbing matters. The problem revolved around conflicting values—Mrs. B.'s concern with the religious vs. the natural significance of children. When value conflicts are particularly distressing, as in this case, it is to be expected that any open confrontation will provoke anxiety. On the assumption that the counselee has normal mental health and in view of the time limitations usually placed on the religious counselor, focusing such a dialogue can be a most effective procedure.

Clarification of Value Conflicts

A second approach to value counseling is the procedure of clarification.[10] Since we often acquire our values through identifications in childhood rather than through rational choice, we are sometimes "fuzzy" about the nature of these values and the effect they have on our actions. Many people need the opportunity to define their values in a dialogue.

> *Mary:* The black students in our school are really asserting themselves. They took over the student assembly today and tried to tell us what we have to do. I don't have any race prejudice but I get mad when people do things like that.

> *Counselor:* You must have been pretty upset by it all.

> *Mary:* I sure was. They have no right telling us what we should do. After all, there are only fifty of them in the whole school and they get the worst grades in the school.

> *Counselor:* In some way they are inferior to the rest of the school.

> *Mary:* That is not so. I look on all people as created equal by God. It makes no difference whether they are white, yellow, brown, or black. I just don't like people pushing other people around, especially if they're black.

> *Counselor:* "Especially if they're black"—you consider all people equal but somehow if they are black, they don't measure up to the rest of us.

Mary: I really never thought that I felt any prejudice against black people, but I have never had the opportunity to associate with them much. Before I came to this school, I had never talked to one. Maybe I do have some prejudice after all. My mother certainly can't see Negroes for dust. Even now she would have a fit if she thought I was associating with them at school.

Counselor: M-hm.

Mary: Maybe in one way I think that all people are equal and in another way I think that they are not.

During this dialogue the counselee clarifies her values relating to the equality of races. By examining her feelings, she begins to realize that her values in this instance are not what she thought them to be.

Self-Revelation

Frequently a counselee believes in certain values but finds them extremely difficult to follow. The opportunity to discuss this situation with another person clears the air and makes the consequences of a decision more tolerable.

Pete: I dropped around to discuss my divorced state with you. I have been divorced a year now and find living almost unbearable.

Pastor: M-hm (and nods).

Pete: I get terribly lonesome. I sometimes feel like tossing it all over and getting married again.

Pastor: You must get pretty disgusted at times.

Pete: Yes, I really get depressed, but my faith means everything to me. I just could not go on without it. I know that the Church won't let me get married again. After all, I am the one who made the mistake.

Pastor: You feel that you're in a real bind. You don't think that you can take this single living and yet you can't get married again.

Pete: That is true but I really have to learn to live with this situation if I am going to be true to myself and to God. I could never give up going to Communion. It means too much to me. It would be more of a burden than living the way I do now. I don't think I could go to sleep, knowing that in some way I was excluded from the Church.

Pastor: Since your faith means so much to you, have you ever thought of giving yourself even more to it?

Pete: What do you mean?

Pastor: Have you ever thought of getting involved in helping others?

In this instance, the dialogue allows the counselee to see how he really feels and the self-revelation has a mitigating effect.[11] He can take a better look at the alternatives and make a more decisive choice. The pastor's suggestion that he become even more committed to his belief is intended to strengthen the decision further.

We have considered the nature, scope, and purpose of religious counseling as well as some possible approaches to the counseling dialogue. Let us now discuss the characteristics of one of the parties in the dialogue, the clergyman.

References

[1] William Schofield, *Psychotherapy: The Purchases of Friendship* (Englewood Cliffs, N.J.: Prentice-Hall, Inc., 1964).

[2] Stephen C. Pepper, *The Source of Value* (Berkeley: University of California Press, 1956).

[3] Elizabeth D. Hurlock, *Child Development*, 4th ed. (New York: McGraw-Hill Book Company, 1964), pp. 548–49.

[4] Ira J. Gordon, *Human Development* (New York: Harper & Row, Publishers, 1962), pp. 318–21.

[5] Donald D. Glad, *Operational Values in Psychotherapy* (New York: Oxford University Press, Inc., 1959).

[6] Leona E. Tyler, *The Work of the Counselor* (New York: Appleton-Century-Crofts, 1961).

[7] Leona E. Tyler, *Counselor's Approaches to Developmental Changes of Values in Clients*, Three Joint Symposia from the ACPA–APA Meetings of 1957, 1958, 1959 (New York: Fordham University, American Catholic Psychological Association, 1960), pp. 165–71.

[8] *Ibid.*, pp. 169–70.

9 Lewis R. Wolberg, *The Technique of Psychotherapy*, Part I (New York: Grune & Stratton, Inc., 1967), pp. 427–29.

10 Kenneth M. Colby, *A Primer of Psychotherapists* (New York: The Ronald Press Company, 1951), pp. 83–86.

11 Sidney M. Jourard, *Disclosing Man to Himself* (Princeton, N.J.: D. Van Nostrand Co., Inc., 1968).

5

The Counselor
as a Person

The counselor's personality is one of his most important assets as he helps the counselee pursue a happy life.[1] Theorists in counseling agree that the personality of the counselor can determine his success or failure.[2] The counselor gives something human and intangible to the counselee which permits him to grow or to change, but theorists have not yet defined exactly what the counselor gives.[3] Dr. Tyler says, "successful outcomes seem to depend as much on what the counselor is as on what he says or does." [4]

Each clergyman has unique characteristics which largely determine the way the counselee responds during the interview. If the counselor is a warm, friendly person, his effect on the counselee will be different from that of a quiet, austere person. The importance of personality raises the question of what kind of a person makes an ideal counselor: an extrovert who feels at ease with people and reaches out to them; an introvert who is highly sensitive to people's inner experiences; a well-balanced, stable person who can avoid emotional pitfalls; or a person who has experienced anxiety, conflict, and indecision in his own life and can understand these feelings in other people. Dr. Tyler has suggested that there is no single type of person who makes an effective counselor, just as there is no single type of man who makes a successful husband, father, or neighbor.[5] If we are looking for an underlying quality, she suggests that it is a capacity for forming deep, vital relationships with other people. Aside from this suggestion, research has yet to come up with any specific types of personalities that are ideal for counseling. Anyone with adequate intelligence and a personality that is sincere and open can in all probability learn to be a good counselor. In fact, successful religious counselors come from many backgrounds and possess a variety of personality traits. If we were to look for a common denominator, we might suggest that the religious counselor be a person who not only feels at ease in relating to others but also has the capacity to show his "real self."

Congruence

Although researchers have been unable to describe the ideal personality for counseling, they do suggest specific qualities which appear to contribute significantly to success or failure. Rogers says the counselor should possess *congruence;* he means that the counselor should manifest no contradiction between what he is and what he says.[6] A good counselor is genuine; he does not play a role intended to impress the counselee.[7] He knows how he feels about the counselee and about the matter under discussion, although he may not think it appropriate at the moment to state his feelings directly. He does not try to hide them or to pretend that he feels otherwise. For example, the clergyman who listens to a pretty young mother telling him that her husband has maltreated her physically and has failed to support their children may very well experience strong protective feelings and sexual attraction. If he possesses personality congruence he will be aware of these feelings and realizes that they can influence his view of the counselee and her situation. He does not fear or deny these feelings but admits that they are affecting his relationship with the counselee. Because he has congruence, he can offer constructive help.

The counselor who lacks congruence proceeds as if his feelings did not exist, perhaps behaving as an ardent champion of a wronged member of the opposite sex. He assumes toward the counselee the role of a father sympathizing with an afflicted daughter. He affects a pseudowarmth, thinking that he is being himself, whereas he may actually be reflecting the way he felt as a child when his father was brutal to his mother. If he does not allow himself to look at the situation objectively his counseling may have a detrimental effect on the counselee.

Self-Acceptance

Self-acceptance is another characteristic of the good religious counselor.[8] The individual who is unable to accept himself is usually quite defensive and alert to protect the vulnerable aspects of his personality. He finds it very difficult to be himself with other people because he fears that they will eventually hurt him. As a consequence he often assumes an artificial manner. He may, for example, give the impression of complete self-assurance and composure even in the most trying circumstances. He may have used this defense for so long that it has become a part of himself; he may not even be aware that he is using it. Although in reality he feels inadequate, he maintains an air of complete self-confidence. Sooner or later the counselee sees through the defense, loses confidence in the counselor, and gains little further benefit from the counseling.

Self-Knowledge and Self-Love

Self-acceptance implies self-knowledge and self-love. The person who accepts himself has acquired, through experience, a knowledge of his usual ways of thinking, feeling, and acting. He recognizes and can accept both his assets and his limitations, his good points and his defects.[9] For example, he may have a sharp, creative mind but at the same time show a tendency to become morose and irritable. He does not deny that he has this personal characteristic but tries to offset it or "live around it." Self-love springs from this self-knowledge and self-acceptance. One of the precepts of Jesus Christ is that one should love his neighbor as himself. (A presupposition of this statement is that one loves himself; he cannot otherwise love his neighbor or open himself to other people.) The person who hates himself is usually self-centered; he directs much of his attention toward the characteristics that he detests in himself, or he builds a protective wall around himself so that neither he nor anyone else can see what he considers hateful. If he follows either of these courses, he closes himself off from love of other people. The person who loves himself can look at his loveable qualities and having recognized these can look outside himself and see loveable qualities in other people.

Personal Holiness

Another major characteristic of the religious counselor is personal holiness. The counselee seeks out the clergyman because of the faith he represents. He expects to meet a person with special qualifications, particularly a total dedication to God. Even though the counselee may wish to discuss a matter not directly connected with religion, he expects the religious counselor somehow to give it a religious perspective. To see the religious dimension demands a deep faith and an awareness of the divine presence in every aspect of one's life. The religious counselor must be a man of God, open to the workings of the Spirit, if he expects God to work through him to enlighten the counselee. Religious counseling, therefore, requires that the counselor integrate Christianity into his personality and pursue a cultivated spiritual life. He should be a thoroughly convinced Christian. If he is half-hearted in his belief, he can hardly expect to lead others in their pursuit of a Christian life. He may become a good counselor, but he will never become a good *Christian* counselor.

As we have said, a primary source of values is identification with people whom we respect.[10] The child assumes the values of his parents because he loves and respects them. The same thing often happens with the individual who comes to a religious counselor. The counselor who lives his Christianity cannot help but reflect his values during the interview. Often, because he is engaged in Christian counseling, he may deliberately set forth his religious beliefs. At other times he may not mention them explicitly but may reveal them in some indirect manner. Even though the counselee may not be aware of the full extent of the counselor's faith and dedication, he may gain a certain inspiration from the counselor's example and try to imitate his values.

Other Qualities
of the Good Counselor

From their research on the qualities that differentiate the good counselor from the poor one, Combs and Soper have defined a number of desirable characteristics that are linked with perceptual organization.[11] The good counselor functions more from an internal than an external frame of reference. He is sensitive to the way things look to other people. Instead of evaluating their acts, he is interested in how they think, feel, and perceive the events about them. He thinks about people in personal rather than impersonal terms.

As we have previously stated, the effective counselor has a healthy attitude toward himself. He knows he is an acceptable member of mankind and does not withdraw or set himself apart from people. He identifies with other people. As a consequence, he is self-revealing rather than self-concealing, willing to be himself and to see the importance of his doubts and shortcomings. He tends to view events in a broad rather than a narrow perspective, seeing the larger connotations instead of getting bogged down in the details.

The good counselor is a friendly person who regards other people as friendly and interesting. Because he has accepted himself, he looks upon others as well-intentioned rather than threatening. For him other people have a dignity and integrity which must be respected; no one is unimportant or worthless. He is motivated by altruism rather than narcissism.

In his approach to the counseling session, the effective counselor regards the counselee as a dependable person who has the capacity to deal with his own problems. He has faith in the counselee and shows confidence in his stability and reliability. He is not suspicious of his motives. He sees as the purpose of counseling the promotion of personal freedom and does not control, dominate, coerce, or manipulate the counselee.

Transference and Countertransference

One of the chief phenomena in psychoanalytic therapy is transference. This term applies to the process "whereby the patient expresses feelings and attitudes that he formerly experienced in reference to some important person or persons in his past life." [12] He unconsciously "transfers" or projects these feelings on to the therapist. Thus, the love or hate that was once directed toward his father is now turned toward the psychoanalyst. Apparently transference sometimes occurs in situations other than formal analysis. Some authorities claim that transference occurs and must be dealt with in counseling, whereas others, like Carl Rogers, see little evidence of it in the counseling situation.[13] This diversity of opinion might stem from the fact that some counselors actually encourage transference, whereas others, especially if they are client-centered in their orientation, try to avoid it. Wherever the truth lies, there seems to be little doubt that transference is not limited just to psychotherapy and sometimes enters into counseling. Counselees fear the counselor, depend on him, love him, or hate him without any obvious, realistic reason. A depth analysis often shows that these responses have their roots in previous interpersonal experiences which are now transferred to the counselor. It is not unusual for the religious counselor to become the object of a parishioner's seemingly unfounded anger and hostility; the source of this reaction may be a displacement of feelings from an authoritarian, domineering father to the counselor, who stands in the position of a Godly father. Making use of transference feelings is a highly technical aspect of psychoanalysis, requiring considerable understanding and skill, and it thus falls outside the scope of religious counseling.[14] The clergyman needs to realize when the phenomenon of transference is taking place, so that he can accept these feelings of the counselee for what they are and not block their release by being overcritical.

A reaction which has greater significance for the religious counselor is countertransference. In this instance, the counselor projects on the counselee "revived elements of attitudes, misconceptions, fears, and impulses derived from his own emotionally significant past."[15] The counselee's appearance, gestures, mannerisms, or personality traits prompt the counselor to act in an unrealistic way. For example, the religious counselor may be more than usually attracted to a young woman who is quite ordinary in appearance but whose mannerisms are similar to those of a much-loved younger sister. Irritation, hostility, and boredom as well as spontaneous attraction are possible signs of countertransference. A countertransference reaction can include the counselor's conscious or unconscious responses toward real or imagined attitudes and behavior of the counselee.[16]

The causes of countertransference are threefold: (1) the counselor's unresolved problems; (2) situational pressures; (3) excessive sympathy for the feelings of the counselee.[17] In the first instance, the counselor because of personal anxiety responds to a certain type of counselee or to a particular topic with hostility and irritation or with excessive sympathy and tenderness. The counselee or the situation has hit the counselor's personality "weak spot." For example, the clergyman whose father was a confirmed alcoholic and bully finds himself edgy and tense every time he is called upon to counsel an alcoholic parishioner. He perhaps does not realize how disturbed he is by this type of counseling experience.

In the second instance, the counselor is merely responding to the many pressures of his working day. He has been rushed and harried from the early hours of the morning and has had a disagreement with his bishop; he walks into the rectory parlor to confront a scrupulous, discontented forty-year-old woman who is bent on committing suicide. Without realizing it, he finds himself pushing for immediate action and change of attitude but meeting only with a frustrating stream of despondent thoughts.

And, in the final instance, the counselor allows himself to absorb the counselee's emotional life. He becomes overly sympathetic and reacts to the counselee's anxiety with a similar anxiety, thus heightening the counselee's stress.

Wolberg suggests several questions a counselor might ask himself to determine whether he is falling into the trap of countertransference.[18]

1. How do I feel about the counselee?
2. Do I anticipate seeing him?
3. Do I overidentify with or feel sorry for him?
4. Do I feel any resentment or jealousy toward him?
5. Do I get extreme pleasure out of seeing him?
6. Do I feel bored with him?
7. Am I fearful of him?
8. Do I want to protect, reject, or punish him?
9. Am I impressed by him?

Should any of the answers point to problems, the counselor should ask himself why such attitudes and feelings exist. Is the counselee doing anything to stir them up? Does the counselee resemble anyone the counselor knows or has known and, if so, are any feelings being transferred to the counselee that are really related to the other person? What role does the counselor want to play with the counselee? Recognizing that he feels angry, displeased, disgusted, irritated, provoked, uninterested, unduly attentive, upset, or overly attracted may suffice to bring these emotions under control. If these reactions persist, then the counselor should himself seek counseling.

The Counselor's Needs

All of us have psychological needs which demand fulfillment. Some of these needs are more pressing than others; some we fulfill, whereas others go unsatisfied. For example, we all have the need to receive attention and recognition from others. Most of us are satisfied if a friend or a superior gives us an occasional sign of approval. The neurotic has needs that are more demanding and unrealistic; the usual signs of affection fail to satisfy him. He wants still more. As a result, he spends a large part of his life looking for attention and recognition.

If a counselor has neurotic needs, he probably takes them into the interview session. Just as he is constantly seeking to fulfill his needs in his everyday life, so he also seeks to fulfill them through the counselee. Quite unconsciously he leads the counselee into a discussion of topics that will cater to his own needs. Some counselors actually enter the profession in the hope of satisfying their inordinate need for acceptance or for domination and protection of others. The counselor with neurotic needs places endless demands upon the counselee and cultivates the counselee's dependence on him.

Some counselors have sexual needs that are neither fulfilled nor sublimated. These needs manifest themselves in the counseling session by an exceptional interest in sexual topics. The counselor, using the counseling session as a means of vicarious satisfaction, unconsciously leads the counselee into detailed accounts of his sexual experiences and derives a certain enjoyment from these accounts. Other counselors reveal their insecurity through an inordinate need for signs of approval. They constantly want to know how much the counselee appreciates their help. To increase the possibility of praise, they go out of their way to appear warm, friendly, and personally concerned. They avoid anything that might antagonize the counselee in the least. If they do not receive the approval they seek, they become depressed and think that they have failed.

The purpose of counseling is to help the counselee, not the counselor. Although the counselor may grow personally as a result of his counseling experiences, this should not be the reason why he engages in counseling.[19] When counseling is merely a means for him to fulfill a neurotic need, it ceases to be counseling and becomes exploitation. Since all of us have at least the tendency toward neuroticism, it behooves us, if we wish to be successful counselors, to be on the alert for manifestations of this condition. If we are aware of its presence, we can take measures to see that it does not impede our effectiveness.

Integrated Personality

Ideally the clergyman who engages in religious counseling should feel that most of his psychological needs have been fulfilled. His peace of mind and relative contentment will reflect the satisfaction of his inner needs. We shall now consider briefly the most important of these needs.

The first is the need to be an integrated person with a sense of identity.[20] There is a tendency among some of the clergy to lead a somewhat schizophrenic life. They govern their existence partially but not completely by the abstract concepts and principles learned in philosophy and theology courses. Intellectually they are clergymen, but emotionally they have failed to assimilate their philosophical and theological principles into their personalities. They have failed to make these principles the core of their philosophy of life. They hold to the basic tenets of Christianity but lack a total conviction and dedication. They accept Christianity fully on an intellectual level but only partially on an emotional and affective level. When they function as counselors they are likely to regard themselves as professional rather than religious counselors. They have yet to integrate the role of clergyman with that of counselor and to see the ways—aside from technical training—in which they differ from the secular counselor. Unless they develop a realization of their identity as religious people in the capacity of counselor, they will not become religious counselors; in many instances they will simply function as second rate psychologists or marriage counselors.

Acceptance and Love

We shall consider second the need for acceptance and love. This need is more likely to present a problem for the priest who is called to a celibate life than for the married clergyman. The priest, whatever he may think, is no more above such a need than anyone else. He needs interpersonal relationships which make him feel understood and wanted. He needs to trust people and to give and receive love. The limitations of celibacy do not dismiss all need for acceptance and love. If the clergyman isolates himself and attempts to live without interpersonal relationships, he will probably experience acute loneliness. If he fails to develop meaningful and satisfying friendships, he may try to fill this need through his relationships with counselees, thereby encouraging dependency in them.

Achievement

Third is the need for achievement and accomplishment. We all need to feel that we are accomplishing something with our lives. If we feel that nothing is resulting from our efforts, we begin to experience a sense of emptiness. The clergyman who is engaged in counseling needs to experience some success in his work and to know that he is accomplishing something worthwhile; otherwise he may become disenchanted and may resort to playing a role.

Some people have a neurotic need to succeed and cannot tolerate failure in any form. If such an individual happens to be a religious counselor, success in counseling is probably all-important to him. He may push constantly for success and act in an excessively directive and authoritarian way. If the counselee does not react as the counselor wishes, he may become very upset. He may overdo his counseling, making himself always available and never thinking of rest or relaxation. He may be constantly on edge and tense but may keep on driving himself, because he finds that counseling fulfills his neurotic need for achievement and accomplishment.

Like the trained psychotherapist, the religious counselor should realize that in some cases he is going to fail. He should be humble enough to admit that there will be some individuals he cannot help. He should learn how to make referrals to other people who are better equipped to help the particular counselee.

Most clergymen have enough success in counseling to fulfill their basic need for achievement and accomplishment. As they become more adept in their counseling, they feel more secure in this function and can tolerate failure more easily. Each success heightens their interest and improves their ability to form counseling relationships.

Work and Rest

At this point we should point out the need for rest and relaxation in the life of a religious counselor. A counselor can only work a certain number of hours each day. Although the counselor may not realize it, counseling is exhausting, emotionally demanding work. It requires that the counselor be in good physical and emotional condition; like the athlete, he must keep himself in top shape. The religious counselor would benefit by taking a professional attitude towards his work. The psychiatrist and clinical psychologist keep set hours for their work; the religious counselor should do the same. In general, he should not establish the practice of seeing people who happen to drop by during his off-duty hours or on his day off.

Perhaps what has been said up to now might cause one to throw up his hands in despair; he might easily conclude that religious counseling requires the counselor to be a paragon of emotional stability and maturity. Actually this kind of counseling requires only normal mental health and an awareness of one's emotional weak spots.[21] No one is devoid of personality limitations; most of us carry the psychological scars of the past. Those who engage in counseling are asked to recognize the ways in which their limitations influence their thinking and acting so as to avoid projecting their own personality deficiencies into the interview and twisting or distorting what the counselee is trying to convey.

Carl Rogers has proposed an excellent set of questions to stimulate self-evaluation.[22] If one makes allowances for the differences between psychological counseling and religious counseling, these questions can be of considerable value to the priest or minister engaged in counseling. At the beginning of each counseling relationship, Rogers asks himself:

1. Can I *be* in some way which will be perceived by the other person as trustworthy, as dependable or consistent in a deep sense. . . ?

2. Can I be expressive enough as a person that what I am will be communicated unambiguously. . . ?

3. Can I let myself experience positive attitudes toward this other person—attitudes of warmth, caring, liking, interest, respect. . . ?

4. Can I be strong enough as a person to be separate from the other? Can I be a sturdy respecter of my own feelings, my own needs, as well as his? Can I own and, if need be, express my own feelings as something belonging to me and separate from his feelings? Am I strong enough in my own separateness that I will not be downcast by his depression, frightened by his fear, nor engulfed by his dependency?

5. Am I secure enough within myself to permit his separateness? Can I permit him to be what he is—honest or deceitful, infantile or adult, despairing or overconfident? Can I give him the freedom to be. . . ?

6. Can I let myself enter fully into the world of his feelings and personal meanings and see these as he does? Can I step into

his private world so completely that I lose all desire to evaluate or judge it. . . ?

7. Can I receive him as he is? Can I communicate this attitude? Or can I receive him only conditionally, accepting some aspects of his feelings and silently or openly disapproving of others. . . ?

8. Can I act with sufficient sensitivity in the relationship that my behavior will not be perceived as a threat. . . ?

9. Can I free him from the threat of external evaluation. . . ?

10. Can I meet this other individual who is in the process of *becoming*, or will I be bound by his past and by my past. . . ?

These questions reflect a deep respect for the dignity and individuality of the counselee. They may be difficult to answer, but even if they remain only half-answered they force the counselor to look within himself and to see what he contributes as a person to the counseling relationship. If the religious counselor can be open and honest with himself, he can offset many of the limitations of his personality.

References

[1] Robert L. Katz, *Empathy: Its Nature and Uses* (New York: The Macmillan Company, 1963), p. 129.

[2] D. H. Ford and H. B. Urban, *Systems of Psychotherapy: A Comparative Study* (New York: John Wiley & Sons, Inc., 1963).

[3] C. P. McGreevy, "Factor Analysis of Measures Used in the Selection and Evaluation of Counselor Education Candidates," *Journal of Counseling Psychology,* XIV (1967), 51–56.

[4] Leona E. Tyler, *The Work of the Counselor,* p. 239.

[5] Tyler, *op. cit.,* p. 246.

[6] Carl R. Rogers, "A Theory of Therapy, Personality and Interpersonal Relationships, as Developed in the Client-Centered Framework," in *Psychology: A Study of Science* (Vol. 3), ed. Sigmund Koch (New York: McGraw-Hill Book Company, 1959).

[7] K. M. Colby, *The Primer of Psychotherapists,* p. 19.

[8] L. M. Brammer and E. L. Shostrom, *Therapeutic Psychology* (Englewood Cliffs, N.J.: Prentice-Hall, Inc., 1960).

[9] Cecil H. Patterson, *Theories of Counseling and Psychotherapy* (New York: Harper & Row, Publishers, 1966).

[10] James C. Coleman, *Personality Dynamics and Effective Behavior* (Chicago: Scott, Foresman & Company, 1960), pp. 303–10.

[11] Arthur W. Combs and Daniel W. Soper, "The Perceptual Organization of Effective Counselors," *Journal of Counseling Psychology*, X (1963), 222–26.

[12] Brammer and Shostrom, *op. cit.*, pp. 210–11.

[13] *Ibid.*, pp. 213–14.

[14] André Godin, S.J., *The Pastor as Counselor* (New York: Holt, Rinehart & Winston, Inc., 1965), p. 79.

[15] Lewis R. Wolberg, *The Technique of Psychotherapy*, Part II (New York: Grune and Stratton, Inc., 1967), p. 749.

[16] Brammer and Shostrom, *op. cit.*, p. 221.

[17] *Ibid.*, pp. 222–23.

[18] L. R. Wolberg, *op. cit.*, p. 754. Quoted by permission of Grune & Stratton, Inc.

[19] *Ibid.*, p. 151.

[20] J. C. Coleman, *op. cit.*, p. 80.

[21] K. M. Colby, *op. cit.*, p. 25.

[22] Carl R. Rogers, "Characteristics of a Helping Relationship," *Personnel and Guidance Journal*, XXXVII (1958), 6–16.

6

Empathy and Acceptance

One of the chief qualities of the good counselor is empathy, a characteristic which allows him to comprehend how the counselee thinks and feels. Empathy is related to the German *einfühlung* which means "feeling into."[1] A father may empathize with an adolescent daughter's sadness and anger after being jilted; he does not feel the same way but he is able to understand and accept what his daughter is experiencing. He implicitly says "I see how you feel." Webster defines empathy as "the imaginative projection of a subjective state whether affective, conative or cognitive into the object so that the object appears to be infused with it." In other words empathy is a capacity of the perceiver to intuit another person's feelings or thoughts.[2]

Of course, the empathetic counselor cannot enter physically the mind or being of another person. He can, however, concentrate his attention on the situation and circumstances described by the counselee and imagine how he would react in similar circumstances.

The counselor can find in himself the feelings and emotions which are associated with the counselee's situation.[3] Some people maintain that through intuition the counselor can even experience partially what another person is experiencing. Although there has been no scientific verification of intuition, it is generally accepted by psychologists as a real aspect of human personality.[4]

In speaking of empathy, Gordon Allport says: "Some people seem by nature to be concerned with the significance of subjective states—with inner feelings, fantasies, wishes, and meanings. They are particularly sensitive to the shadings of motivation, conflict, and sufferings in others.[5]

In effect, the empathetic counselor says:

> To be of assistance to you, I will put aside myself—the self of ordinary interaction—and enter into your world of perception as completely as I am able. I will become, in a sense, another self for you, an alter ego of your attitudes and feelings—a safe opportunity for you to discern yourself more clearly, to experience yourself more truly and more deeply, to choose more significantly.[6]

One of the main characteristics of the empathetic person is an attitude of "otherness."[7] This attitude differs from the process used in making inferences. The counselor who relies on inference analyzes the various factors in a situation, examines the relationships among them, and judges how the counselee should think, feel, or react. He concentrates more on the relationships than on the person. He is "thinking about" instead of "thinking and feeling with" the counselee. "To be truly acquainted with a person means to be able to take his point of view, to think with his frame of reference, and to reason from his premises."[8] The empathetic person momentarily loses his awareness of himself and moves freely into the perceptual field of the counselee.[9]

Another way of approaching the phenomenon of empathy is to distinguish between the internal frame of reference and the external one. The counselor who adopts the external frame of reference concentrates on causes and reasons for the counselee's problem. He says to himself: "This man has a difficult problem. I wonder what caused it? How can I help him?" The counselor who adopts the internal frame of reference tries to put himself in the counselee's place: "You are very disturbed by this situation and want to do something about it." At the same time he may say to himself: "I must try to understand how he looks at this problem and to help him clarify his thinking about it so that he can make a decision."[10] He makes a concerted effort "to get under the skin" of the counselee and to relive his thoughts and feelings.[11]

A good description of empathy can be found in Harper Lee's *To Kill a Mockingbird*. Atticus, the sagacious lawyer, tells Scout, his seven-year-old daughter, who has come to him with complaints about the unfairness of other people, to "get into their shoes and walk around in them." He then suggests that if she had the same problem and attitude as the person who drew the complaint, she would probably act in the same way.

Empathy can sometimes occur in the act of literary appreciation. Occasionally one finds an authority on the works of a renowned author who has not only read, comprehended, and absorbed his writings, but has also "gotten into the mind" of the author. He has fully apprehended the author's internal frame of reference and has achieved a rare appreciation of the man and his works. Another person may have read just as much but may never really know the author as thoroughly. One has experienced an empathy that the other lacks. Similarly, the effective counselor has managed "to get into the mind" of the counselee.

Attributes of
the Empathetic Person

People differ in their ability to empathize. Some have an inborn gift; others, though limited in natural insight, develop a sufficient capacity for empathy to become effective counselors. Proficiency is related to intelligence, experience, and maturity.[12] It also demands detachment and insight into oneself.[13] The empathetic counselor does not allow himself to become entangled in the emotional life of the counselee. He generally has sufficient self-understanding to recognize his own emotional weakspots and the types of situations that may disturb him. As a result, he knows when he is becoming too involved and takes steps to disentangle himself. He realizes that too much sympathy can be harmful, since it lessens his objectivity and makes him concentrate on one area of conflict at the expense of others.

Empathy calls for a natural appreciation of nuances of behavior.[14] The counselor takes note of verbal and nonverbal cues that other people often overlook. He has an openness of mind which allows him to detect signs of anxiety and hostility and to project himself into the world of the counselee. He is not afraid of disturbing feelings and emotions nor does he avoid speaking about matters which evoke such feelings. He also recognizes and accepts his inner conflicts and as a consequence does not allow them to limit his capacity for empathy. This openness to self allows him to receive the message as it is intended by the counselee, without filtering or diverting it. His personal experiences with either typical or atypical problems of living have been sufficiently understood and accepted to make them positive rather than negative assets. He knows how the counselee must be reacting to a particular situation because he himself has passed through a similar experience or has had similar feelings.

"As If" Frame of Mind

In those instances when he has not had a similar reaction, the counselor can often imagine the counselee's feelings by assuming an "as if" frame of mind.[15] Because of his reading and his experience with other counselees, he can reconstruct a person's reaction to certain situations. This imaginative projection demands creativity and mental alertness. Some counselors practice the "as if" way of thinking by asking themselves, either during or immediately after a counseling session, "How would a person in the counselee's age-bracket and with his background react when placed in the situation he describes?"

Although empathetic people usually relate well with others, they are not necessarily extroverts. They show a warm but not aggressive interest in other people. Strange as it may seem, research shows that many empathetic people are dependent conformists, while many unempathetic people are dominating and independent.[16]

One of the main characteristics of the empathetic person is spontaneity. He is a relaxed, "human" person,[17] one who is not restricted to a particular technique or method. Unfortunately, some counselors lose their naturalness and defeat their purpose by trying to imitate slavishly the technique of an authority.[18]

Developing understanding and empathy can be compared to learning to play a piano. Almost anyone can learn the mechanics and achieve some success, but only those with talent can give a genuinely artistic performance. The outstanding pianist has an elusive quality over and above technical skill that distinguishes him from other pianists. Some counselors are naturally endowed with such sensitivity, warmth, and humanity that they can achieve excellent results with little formal training; others, after making use of every means available to heighten their empathic ability, still may have only moderate success. Most counselors can develop some proficiency, if they make an effort to achieve greater self-understanding and objectivity. It should be kept in mind, however, that even the most empathetic person can only approximate the thought patterns, feelings, and attitudes of another person.[19] Fortunately even a partial comprehension is enough to help the counselee understand the realities of his situation.

Personality and Empathy

Success at being empathetic is sometimes dependent on the counselor's knowledge of the personality and immediate situation of the counselee. There are some with whom we can empathize quite easily, others with whom it is more difficult. In general, we empathize more readily with those whom we find attractive and similar to ourselves.[20] The more an individual likes a person, the more he assumes that this person thinks and feels as he does.[21] The closer the value system to one's own, the greater the chance for empathy.[22] Men empathize better with other men, and women with other women. With considerable experience, however, some men become quite proficient at empathizing with women and vice versa. For example, some women high school teachers achieve considerable success in understanding adolescent boys, while some clergymen become highly effective in empathizing with women. The more an individual knows about another, the better he will be able to empathize. One cannot understand the inner world of another person unless he has adequate information about that world. Finally, the counselee's external situation affects the empathy of the counselor. A knowledge of the detailed circumstances producing the problem helps the counselor to comprehend the counselee's inner reaction.

Hindrances to Empathy

Learning to empathize is an easily hindered task.[23] Language differences, for example, can present a major obstacle—not only differences in native language but also differences in proficiency within the same language. Frequently the counselor is a better educated person than the counselee, and sometimes the disparity is very great. Because of a limited educational background, the counselee may understand and use English quite differently from the counselor. The counselor must try to comprehend the counselee's way of speaking if he is to understand his inner world.

Differences in age and experience constitute other obstacles. As the counselor gets further from his adolescent years, he often finds it more difficult to understand the teen-age mind. Similarly, the young counselor frequently has trouble empathizing with the aged counselee, as he has not experienced personally the problems facing old people. The reaction of a counselee who has lived through the horrors of a war, an experience which is completely unknown to the counselor, can present an enigma. Hence, the wider the experiential range of the counselor, the more likely it is that he will achieve empathy. As a partial substitute for actual experience, vicarious experience gained from reading novels or attending plays can sometimes be helpful.

The personality of the counselor can also become an obstacle to empathy. Fears, unmet needs, and unresolved personal problems can raise a wall of anxiety between the counselor and the counselee.[24] Insecurity and rigidity distort the empathic relationship, by forcing the counselor to become defensive.[25] Instead of giving his attention to what is taking place in the session, the anxious counselor stays on the alert for the slightest word that might further diminish his already depleted self-esteem. He is overly sensitive to insinuations, quick to attack and rebuke. He is oblivious of all indications that he has not been effective in reaching the counselee. As a result, the counselee becomes vaguely aware that what he is trying to say is not getting through. He withdraws his trust and confidence and hunts for a way to terminate the contact gracefully.

Types of Counselors

Counselors with unresolved personal problems often develop ways to hide their limitations.[26] Some do too much talking and too little listening. They rapidly form a judgment about the cause of a problem and then, through persuasion, exhortation, and pleading, they attempt to coerce the counselee into accepting their view. They do not feel successful until the counselee indicates complete agreement and a determination to follow their suggestions.

Other counselors may have a psychological imbalance and may become possessive and overly involved. They merge their own lives with the counselee's, demanding fidelity and confidence. In a real sense, they take over the counselee's life, making him extremely dependent. Their major concern is to keep the relationship alive. They draw their strength and security from the conviction that another person admires and depends upon them. Such counselors are incapable of much empathy. They are too taken up with trying to fulfill their own unmet needs to devote their full attention to the counselee's experiences.

Still other counselors assume a role of silence. They are excellent listeners, but they listen in a passive, sympathetic way. They take delight in having other people flock to them to pour out their hearts, but they never take a stand or show any sign of inner conviction. Like sponges, they soak up other people's troubles. In some instances, nothing more is needed and they are successful; in others, the counselee departs taking little from the counseling experience. Such counselors make an all-out effort to appear friendly and understanding. Actually, they are complacent and will do anything to avoid areas of conflict. They are too threatened to show strength joined with true warmth and humanity. Their capacity for empathy is limited, since they are mainly concerned with creating a front and sedulously avoiding topics touching on their own inner conflicts.

The counselor skilled in empathy is one who possesses both a well-balanced personality and sufficient strength to assert himself when the occasion demands it. He does not become the counselee's doormat but takes a stand when he is convinced that the situation calls for it.[27]

Above all else he is humble and sincere.[28] He is not self-opinionated. When necessary, he can easily put aside his own views in order to grasp the counselee's outlook. He is ready to accept new ideas, even upsetting ones. He is aware of his own shortcomings but sufficiently humble to accept them, without spending his time trying to hide them. He is open to himself and the world about him and consequently to the counselee's world.

Acceptance

After he has acquired an empathy with the counselee, the counselor often feels an acceptance, a deep respect for human worth and dignity. He values each counselee to such an extent that for a time he willingly gives himself to the task of helping him. Several attitudes follow naturally from this respect.[29] First, the counselor recognizes that the counselee has the right to live his own life and make his own decisions. It is not the counselor's function to take over his life; were this true, the counselor would be indicating some doubt about the worth of the counselee. Second, he realizes that almost every individual has the capacity to choose wisely and to live a full, self-directed life. Finally, he recognizes that each person is responsible to God and himself for his own life. Acceptance, therefore, means that the counselor trusts the innate capacities of the counselee and believes that, given an opportunity, the counselee will find within himself or will receive from God the insight he needs to solve his problem and to grow as a Christian.

Acceptance does not mean, however, that the counselor approves of the counselee's views and opinions.[30] Nor does it mean that he approves of his actions, which may at times be sinful. He simply recognizes that the counselee is endowed with freedom to think and act according to his own choice, even though these thoughts and actions may violate the divine law. In effect, the counselor says "I respect you even though I do not agree with your views or approve your actions." In so doing, he centers his attention on the person of the counselee rather than on his ideas or behavior. Although mentally he may disapprove of the way the individual acts, he avoids threatening the counselee by showing his disapproval openly. This does not mean that the counselor is too weak to make known his disapproval or that in reality he approves the action. It simply means that he is mainly concerned with the response of the counselee and is convinced that any indication of disapproval would detract from the effectiveness of his counseling.

Up to this point we have primarily discussed the counselor and his personality. We have seen how his personal qualities and attitudes, particularly his empathy and readiness to accept, can influence the outcome of the counseling. Let us now consider the counselee and the part that he contributes to the process of counseling.

References

[1] Lawrence M. Brammer and E. L. Shostrom, *Therapeutic Psychology* (New York: Prentice-Hall, Inc., 1960), p. 164.

[2] Henry C. Smith, *Sensitivity to People* (New York: McGraw-Hill Book Company, 1966), p. 93.

[3] Henry A. Murray, *Explorations in Personality* (New York: Science Editions, 1962), pp. 246–47.

[4] *Ibid.*, p. 246.

[5] Gordon W. Allport, *Pattern and Growth in Personality* (New York: Holt, Rinehart & Winston, 1961), p. 511.

[6] Carl R. Rogers, *Client-Centered Therapy* (Boston: Houghton Mifflin Company, 1951), p. 35.

[7] Allport, *op. cit.*, p. 536.

[8] *Ibid.*, p. 542.

[9] Robert L. Katz, *Empathy: Its Nature and Uses* (New York: The Macmillan Company, 1963), p. 140.

[10] Brammer and Shostrom, *op. cit.*, pp. 162–63.

[11] Rogers, *op. cit.*, p. 29.

[12] Allport, *op. cit.*, p. 521.

[13] Katz, *op. cit.*, p. 140.

[14] *Ibid.*, p. 135.

[15] *Ibid.*, p. 144.

[16] June E. Chance and W. Meaders, "Needs and Interpersonal Perception," *Journal of Personality*, XXVIII (1960), 200–210.

[17] Katz, *op. cit.*, p. 158.

[18] *Ibid.*, p. 176.

19 *Ibid.* p. 143.

20 Allport, *op. cit.,* pp. 516–17.

21 E. Stotland, A. Zander, and T. Natsoulas, "Generalization of Interpersonal Similarity," *Journal of Abnormal and Social Psychology,* LXII (1961), 250–56.

22 Allport, *op. cit.,* p. 543.

23 Brammer and Shostrom, *op. cit.,* p. 164.

24 Katz, *op. cit.,* p. 167.

25 Dominick A. Barbara, *The Art of Listening* (Springfield, Ill.: Charles C. Thomas, Publisher, 1958), p. 3.

26 Barbara, *op. cit.,* pp. 160–63.

27 Michael E. Cavanagh, "Personalism is Not Patientism: A Philosophical Position Applied to Psychotherapy," *The American Journal of Psychiatry,* CXXII, No. 12 (1966), 1443–45.

28 Barbara, *op. cit.,* p. 63.

29 Brammer and Shostrom, *op. cit.,* pp. 157–58.

30 *Ibid.,* p. 159.

7

The Experiential
World

Each individual represents a unique combination of experiences and perceives the external world of people and objects in a manner that differs from every other person's. Each has thoughts and emotions that are peculiarly his own and acts in a way that is characteristically his. No two people have the same experiences, even when they find themselves in the same circumstances. One of the counselor's first and most important tasks is to use his own personality and experience to enter the experiential world of the counselee. When the counselee can say that the counselor grasps the way he looks at and feels about a personal problem, he will feel that he has at last found someone who understands him— and feeling understood is one beneficial result of counseling.[1]

Religious counseling unites two inner words, that of the counselor and that of the counselee. In attempting to understand the counselee's inner world, the counselor performs a task which at first sight looks self-contradictory. He must for a period of time set aside his own inner world and immerse himself completely in trying to understand the counselee's, yet his insights about the counselee's inner world come mainly from his own experience. The process of empathetic projection already described improves any form of counseling, whether directive and authoritarian or extremely non-directive. Suggestions will be more efficacious if they are given after the counselor understands the problems from the counselee's point of view. Moreover, as we have said, feeling understood gives the counselee the sense of support he needs to look more deeply within himself, to find God, and to reach a solution to or way of living with his problems.

The Counselee's Inner World

What it means to understand the counselee's inner world can be demonstrated by an example and a diagram (cf. Figure 2, p. 76). Let us consider a case history which we can relate to the diagram in order to explain the essential elements involved in this kind of understanding.

Jane is a high school senior and has had Sister Mary as a counselor for the past two years. During this period she has discussed with her several personal and scholastic problems, but she has put off the question of her calling to a dedicated life. When she was in grammar school, she talked of becoming a nun, but gradually the desire slipped away. Recently it has returned and has aroused conflicting emotions.

Jane is the oldest of four girls; her youngest sister is only four. Her parents have finished divorce proceedings within the past year. As long ago as Jane can remember, her parents constantly quarreled; many of the arguments stemmed from her father's alcoholism. Jane has never known a happy family life. Her mother is a weak woman filled with self-pity. She looks to Jane for support and places on her shoulders much of the responsibility of caring for her younger sisters. Jane has always responded to her mother's demands because she feels that she should. In many ways Jane is a slave to her sense of duty. She has done well at school because she thinks she should give good example to her younger sister—and because it makes her mother happy. Her uncle, a man whom she greatly admires, is a priest. Two of her cousins have also chosen a dedicated life in the convent. Since they appear to be very happy, she thinks she should follow in their footsteps.

Even though her mother manifests great regard for priests and nuns, and secretly wishes that she had chosen their way of life, she still does everything she can to dissuade Jane from entering the convent. Jane has enough self-understanding

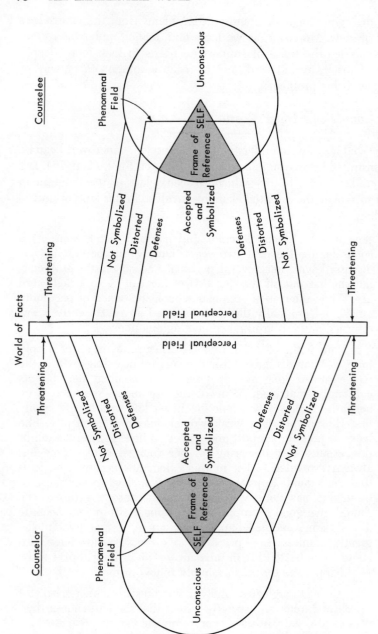

Figure 2. Diagram of the Experiential World of the Counselor and the Counselee.

to realize that she is unhappy and resentful of the role she is forced to assume. As she faces the question of a vocation, she is torn by conflicting feelings. If God is really calling her, then her faith demands that she should answer the call. At the same time, she thinks that she might be trying to escape from an intolerable situation at home, and that since her first obligation is to her mother and sisters she should give up all thought of entering the convent at present.

The counselor's interaction with this counselee can be better understood by analyzing several elements common to both their inner worlds: the objective facts, the perceptual field, the phenomenal field, the frame of reference, the self-concept, the experience of threat, and defensive reactions (Figure 2). The counselor tries to gain some insight into the counselee's phenomenal field and frame of reference or in other words tries to understand what Jane accepts and what she distorts as she perceives the objective facts.[2] Of course the counselor's own frame of reference and phenomenal field will affect her insight.

The starting point in considering this case is the world of facts (Figure 2). This world consists of the people, things, circumstances, and situations that exist in external reality. Some of them are perceived by the counselee; others are passed over unnoticed. The perceptual field includes everything the individual can perceive at any one moment, whether in an accurate or a distorted way.[3] It consists of his perceptions before he colors them according to his own distinctive frame of reference. The perceptual field can widen as the counselee grows more open to experience. For instance, when Jane feels less threatened, she can permit herself to look at things that she never dared previously to examine. More important than objective external reality is the individual's coloring of his perceptual field. As a result of his contact with his environment and with other people, he places positive or negative values on certain experiences.

If the counselor approaches his task from the standpoint of logic, he may think that initially he should concentrate on the facts of the counselee's situation and try to make the counselee come to grips with reality. Often many counselees are too confused and distressed to tackle the world as it actually exists. Since they find a direct confrontation too painful and threatening, they close their eyes to reality or distort it in order to make the world seem more tolerable. In Jane's case, the world of facts existed on two levels, both threatening in some respects. On the purely natural level were her unbearable home life, self-pitying mother, alcoholic father, and —on the more pleasant side—relatives in the religious life who appeared to be happy and content; on the spiritual level was the possibility that God was calling her through special graces to become a nun, a call which would demand that she sacrifice things she greatly desired. At the start of counseling, the most important thing was to understand how Jane perceived her situation. It was Sister Mary's task to discover how Jane felt about entering the convent.

The Phenomenal Field

Each of us views the perceptual field from his own vantage point and creates his personal reality from it.[4] This personal reality constitutes the phenomenal field (Figure 2),[5] the data from the perceptual field that has been interpreted by the conscious and unconscious mind. It provides our internal frame of reference—our personal and unique way of perceiving the world. Rogers says that this phenomenal field "includes all that is experienced by the organism, whether or not these experiences are consciously perceived." He notes that only a small part of this perception is conscious but that "a large portion of this world is available to consciousness." [6]

In forming the phenomenal field, the organism receives impressions from the perceptual field and either 1) accepts and symbolizes them (translates them into thoughts and words); 2) distorts them by using defense mechanisms; or 3) receives them but does not symbolize them (Figure 2). This process of selection, distortion, and rejection depends on the individual's self-concept. Briefly, impressions from the objective world are accepted and symbolized if they are consistent with the self-concept, distorted or rejected if they pose a threat to it or are inconsistent with it, and ignored if they seem to have no connection with it.

Some examples will help to illustrate this process clearly:

> Two men listen to a sermon on God's mercy. They sit side by side in the same church. They hear the same words. For one the sermon is an inspiration; for the other, a terrifying ordeal.

The first has a healthy personality that is receptive to all that has been said; the second is neurotic and burdened with pathological guilt, and as a result completely misses the theme of the sermon. He concentrates on one or two remarks dealing with the evil of sin. The approach of each man to the same situation is determined by his mental state and personality structure.

Combs and Snygg give the example of two men who are driving down a Western road when an object looms up in front of their car.[7] One sees it as a boulder, reacts with fright, and jams on the brakes; the other sees it as a tumbleweed and reacts with complete nonchalance. Both perceive the same outer reality, but each perceives it differently.

The uniqueness of each person's phenomenal field is an important consideration in the counseling process, in which two individuals examine the same data, the matter presented by the counselee. Naturally the counselee sees this matter from his own point of view. A counselor may also look spontaneously at the matter from his own point of view, unless he makes a concerted effort to see it as the counselee does. Since he is not the counselee, his insight will never be perfect, but he can reach an approximation of what the counselee is perceiving. The more he listens to and tries to know the counselee, the closer the approximation. If the counselor limits himself to his own phenomenal field, then it is highly probable that he will offer suggestions that have little meaning for the counselee. If the counselee is frank he will probably complain that the religious counselor does not understand—and he will probably be correct. Understanding the counselee implies that the counselor must recognize and temporarily put aside his personal reactions to the matter in order to comprehend what the counselee is experiencing.

Let us return to Jane and her struggle with a vocation. In the beginning session, Jane presented her view—derived from her phenomenal field—of the dilemma. Sister Mary listened and, because she is an unthreatened, impartial observer with considerable experience in counseling, she probably saw many salient aspects which Jane failed to see. It is true that Sister Mary automatically places what she hears in the framework of her own views and experiences —her own phenomenal field. She could have offered advice on this basis, but then it is likely that the advice would have fit herself and

not Jane. Moreover, Jane was too threatened at the time by the idea
of becoming a nun to face it in a cool, objective manner. Sister Mary
first had to get Jane to talk freely enough about her feelings and
views—her phenomenal field—for her to gain some self-understanding about this possible call from God. As Jane talked about what
she was experiencing—her doubts, hesitations, worries, and fears—
the elements of the problem gradually became clearer and began
to fall in place. She came to accept things that she would never
previously have admitted to herself. With Sister Mary as a patient,
understanding listener, Jane reached the point where she could
admit that her life had been governed by the tyranny of the
"should" and that this "should" was probably influencing her feelings about her vocation. Once she faced this, she could act from
freedom rather than from compulsion. She could then think more
objectively about whether God was truly offering her a special
"calling."

The Frame of Reference

The frame of reference is part of the phenomenal field. On
the basis of past experience, the growing individual develops a
frame of reference which he continues to use during his adult life
(Figure 2).[8] The frame of reference is composed of his assumptions
and attitudes about the world and himself. It colors all that he sees
and hears. For example, the average man develops a frame of
reference that is masculine whereas a woman develops one that is
feminine. A couple may pass a woman wearing the latest style in
hats. The husband does not even notice that the woman is wearing
a hat; yet the wife is so taken with the creation that she sees every
detail. Both are looking at the same thing: the man sees it from a
man's point of view and consequently overlooks it. The wife sees it
from a woman's point of view and consequently notes not only its
presence but even its minute features. The results of these two
frames of references are different interests which determine where a
person focuses his attention.

The Self and Self-Concept

One element of the frame of reference is a person's view of himself.[9] This view gradually evolves during childhood and adolescence
as a result of environmental forces and personal experiences. When

a child is born he has a unique potential. The rest of his life he will continually develop himself. Whether or not he will fulfill his potential depends to a large extent upon environmental factors.

Before a child can develop his potentialities, he must come to some realization of his "self." [10] The infant's concept of self begins with the realization that his body is distinct from his mother's. He later realizes that his body is his own and that he can make it do things; still later he discovers that he can think his own thoughts. Only when the child discovers that he thinks and reacts in a different way from other people does he begin to see himself fully. He finds himself by being different in subtle or obvious ways.

The individual's beliefs about himself gradually become more fixed and eventually develop into his "self-concept." Before a child becomes aware of how others evaluate him, he must first realize that he has a "self." Others are judging or labelling whatever is unique in him. If his concept of the self is weak and undeveloped, he will be molded by what others think and will not learn to express himself. When this occurs the child is forming an inadequate image of himself on the basis of what society expects of him. This kind of reliance on social acceptance or rejection does not allow him to know what the self is like. In this case self-actualization cannot fully take place.

At a very early age, a child begins to judge himself in terms of what others think of him. As the infant interacts with his environment, he gradually builds up concepts about himself in relation to his environment.[11] Initially this self-evaluation is influenced by the important people in his life, like his mother and father. The reflective ability of a small child is too limited to allow him to form any consistent picture of his performance or to assess his worth objectively. Very early in life, the child hears such phrases as "You are a good child" or "You are a naughty boy." Parents convey their attitude to the child through their approval or disapproval. Most children accept their parents' authority and do not question their attitudes. If parents look upon their child as alert and lovable and treat him accordingly, he forms this view of himself; if, on the other hand, they are constantly comparing him with an attractive, brilliant younger sister who does everything right whereas he does everything wrong, it is quite likely that he looks upon himself as an inferior person.

The foundation for one's self-concept is laid through parent-child relationships, but the concept may also depend on one's experiences of success or failure.[12] As a child grows he becomes more proficient in evaluating his performance. He can see for himself that he is a good student or a good athlete. If the foundation of the first few years is not too weak, he gradually begins to change some of his views about himself to fit his experiences. Few people develop a self-concept that accords perfectly with what they actually are; most, however, have a self-concept which is fairly accurate. They can see and accept their strong points as well as their limitations, success as well as failure. They undertake new tasks with a conviction that they can succeed. Self-confidence requires a healthy self-concept.

The Consistent Self

The individual who from early childhood has felt that he is inferior and inadequate has a tendency to cling to this view.[13] When he goes to school he is likely to fail, not because he lacks talent but rather because he is convinced that he can do no better. He is often unable to form friendships with those his own age because he thinks they feel the same way he does about himself. If another child goes out of his way to be friendly, the boy with a poor self-concept may misinterpret the offer of friendship as an attempt to get something from him or simply as a manifestation of pity. In brief, he sets the stage for failure; as a consequence he has few experiences which help to build up his self-concept. He tends to play down or misinterpret the few successes he does have because they are not consistent with his picture of himself. In contrast, the child who has a healthy self-concept gains an increased sense of worth from each new achievement or accomplishment. When he does well at school or forms new friendships, he enhances his self-esteem and gains a more objective view of himself.

The self-concept plays a major part in counseling. To a large extent the counselee's view of himself determines his reaction to his problem. If he has an adequate self-concept, he will probably be able to view his situation objectively and see possible avenues of solution. He will look more easily at his own limitations and see how these have contributed to his present trouble. If, on the other hand, he has a poor self-concept, his evaluation of himself and his problem is likely to be distorted or warped. He may be defensive, guarded, and fearful and may indicate to the religious counselor that he thinks he is a very inferior person.[14] He may feel that the situation is hopeless and that there is nothing that he can do to change it. For this reason the counselor cannot afford to pass lightly over the counselee's feelings about himself. A failure to take the self-concept into consideration presents a barrier to understanding the counselee.

The Self as the Center of Experience

All that the counselee perceives is organized around the self. He is interested in those things in the world that pertain to him; the rest he overlooks. "All perceptions existing in the perceptual field acquire their meaning through relationship to the existing self. It is only when the events are perceived as having some important relationship to the self that they are likely to produce much change in the individual's behavior." [15] Jane's view of her vocation is organized around her view of herself. She approaches this decision from the point of view of its meaning to her as an individual. Since she is a devout Catholic, she regards it as an honor flattering to her ego; at the same time, her somewhat deficient self-concept makes her wonder whether she can live up to the demands of such a life. She considers the various aspects of the sister's life in terms of her own approach to life. She imagines how *she* will look in the religious dress, what work *she* will do, and how *she* will participate in community living. Her approach may be somewhat different from that of a friend who also plans to become a nun. Jane might view working with children in a special way simply because of her unique background.

She refuses to face certain aspects of the religious life directly. They are too threatening to her "self." One of these is the renunciation of marriage and motherhood; another, the severing of an unrecognized dependence on her mother and sisters. A confrontation of her dilemma requires a widening of her perceptual field so that she can consider all the implications of the tensions of celibacy and of her need for dependence. In her present state of emotional stress, she cannot face these disturbing issues.

Frame of Reference
in Counseling

Since understanding the counselee's frame of reference is one
of the most important requirements of effective counseling, let us
return for a moment to this component in the diagram (Figure 2).
The crux of the following marriage case demonstrates how necessary it is for the counselor to comprehend the counselee's frame of
reference before any real communication can take place. Many of
the problems that people encounter in everyday life are the outcome of distorted or unacceptable ways of looking at things.

> Mrs. Y. comes to her pastor, complaining that her marriage is
> "on the rocks" and that she doesn't know what she is going to
> do. She begins by saying that she has three small children and
> that before marriage she was a school teacher. She then talks
> about herself, her husband, and their stormy relationship. She
> is of Italian descent; both of her parents were born in Sicily.
> Her husband is third-generation Irish. She is an effusive, vola-
> tile person; her husband is quiet, reserved, and inhibited. Her
> childhood and adolescence were spent in a large family setting,
> surrounded by aunts, uncles, and cousins in addition to five
> brothers and two sisters. There were frequent arguments and
> fights which at times became quite violent, but they were
> usually followed by reconciliation. Showing anger and hos-
> tility when provoked was simply accepted as a normal part of
> living. Her husband, on the other hand, was the younger of
> two sons. He was raised in a reserved, middle-class home. His
> mother was a very proper person, overly conscious of the im-
> pression she made on others. Her attitude towards her two
> sons was protective. She was suspicious of other people's
> motives and consequently had few friends. She rarely showed
> how she felt and almost never lost her temper.
>
> Even though Mrs. Y. maintains that she and her husband
> are much in love, the marriage has been stormy from the be-
> ginning. When something bothers her she fumes and rants,
> but then she is ready to forget the incident. Her husband
> never says a word during these episodes, even when he is the
> object of her rage. When something bothers him, he tries to
> show no emotion but keeps it all inside. On occasion his inner
> tension becomes intolerable; he blows up over some slight in-

convenience and then goes off and drinks excessively. Mrs. Y. cannot understand how such insignificant incidents can provoke so much anger on his part, since he often fails to show any emotion when much more is at stake. The latest episode was over the children leaving their toys on the kitchen floor and not picking them up before dinner.

After the first session, the pastor suggests that she return with her husband for another talk. She agrees but is not sure whether he will agree to come. He does come, however, and the second session begins with Mrs. Y. angrily listing all her grievances against her husband. Her tirade builds up to a climax and then subsides. Not once during this time does the husband offer a word of defense. He sits looking at her, half-shocked and half-angry. Several times the pastor tries to cut in but without success. When Mrs. Y. is finished he asks how she thinks her husband feels as a result of the things she has just said. She is somewhat surprised at the question and she shrugs her shoulders, saying "I don't know."

As the counseling session progresses, it becomes evident that the two have completely different ways of looking at the world and neither realizes this fact. Their attitude toward showing anger openly is just one of the many differences. For Mrs. Y. "letting off steam" is just a normal, natural part of daily living. She affirms that she does not mean most of what she says during these times. She takes it for granted that her husband understands this. She maintains that if she kept everything pent up inside of her, as her husband does, she would "blow up." Her husband, however, considers the episodes of anger in a totally different light. On the few occasions when his mother showed anger, she meant every word she said and usually refused to speak to him for a couple of days after the incident. Fearing a recurrence of these painful episodes he grew up overly sensitive to the slightest sign of anger. From the beginning of his marriage he has taken every word his wife has said at face value and has brooded over it. He has lived in constant dread of provoking further anger. If he himself expresses any anger in retaliation, he immediately begins to feel guilty, just as he did when he was at home with his mother. This difference has prevailed for ten years with neither party suspecting how the other felt. Once this difference has been pointed out and recognized, the air is cleared and they are able to go on to other differences that require mutual understanding.

In this case two people had different ways of looking at the same everyday situation and neither made any effort to understand the other person's view. The wife interpreted demonstrations of anger according to her frame of reference, which was the result of her upbringing; the husband interpreted the same demonstrations according to his background. These divergent views had an important effect on the way they behaved toward each other.[16] The wife considered that showing anger openly was a healthy, harmless reaction, whereas her husband looked upon it as sinful. As a result she was volatile and uncontrolled and he was inhibited and reserved. She was able to "blow off steam," as she put it, without the slightest qualm of conscience; he could not show any sign of anger without suffering pangs of guilt. He therefore repressed his true feelings until they mounted up to the point of explosion. With each explosion he was overwhelmed by guilt and sought escape through alcohol.

Effective counseling in such a situation requires that the counselor (1) make an all-out effort to grasp the inner experience of both the husband and the wife; (2) realize that neither person is aware of the other's frame of reference; (3) create an atmosphere which will allow them to enter each other's inner world and to see how the other person is reacting to the situation under discussion.

Both the counselor and the counselee have their own phenomenal fields, self-structures, and frames of reference. Usually the counselee describes the part of his phenomenal field that pertains to his reasons for coming for counseling. The counselor should pay careful attention to whatever the counselee says that might offer some clues to his frame of reference. These clues will include such basic things as the counselee's sex, race, nationality, education, religious training, and socioeconomic level. The counselor also needs to notice any subtle remarks that offer information about how the counselee thinks and feels.

In addition to taking cognizance of the counselee's view of things, the counselor should be aware of his own frame of reference (Figure 2). Most important, he needs to recognize that he is (or should be) more open than the counselee. As a consequence, his view is broader and more inclusive. He can see aspects of the problem which are closed to the counselee because they are inconsistent with his self-concept, too threatening, or outside his frame of reference.[17] Dwelling on facts that have no meaning to the counselee is usually pointless, as they "go in one ear and out the other."

The Religious
Frame of Reference

In religious counseling a point of special concern should be that aspect of the frame of reference which involves the counselee's religious beliefs and attitudes. As a consequence of past training and experience, each counselee has his own view of God, the Church, the value of a human being, and life after death, to mention a few of the more evident elements. To gain some understanding of the counselee as a religious person the counselor needs some information about how he views the many facets of his belief. Some counselees are fully committed Christians and are profoundly influenced by their faith. Many signs of their religious convictions appear in their actions and speech. Their belief has become an aspect of their personality and now clearly affects much of their behavior. Other counselees, even those who have had an equal amount of religious training, may give little indication that their belief has made an impact on their everyday lives. They may have some religious faith, but it has failed to alter their frames of reference to any significant extent.

Let us consider briefly the cases of two college freshmen. They come to the University chaplain to talk over sexual experiences with steady dates that for both of them led to pregnancies and disturbing guilt-feelings. One is a fundamentally religious person who has for a time abandoned his convictions in rebellion against an overly strict and demanding religious training; the other states that he is a practicing Catholic but actually knows little about his Church, as he has never had the opportunity to learn more than the basic concepts. Because their attitudes on religion differ, the reactions of the two men differ also, even though both have the same strong feelings of guilt. The first student places the whole episode in a religious context. He is preoccupied with the magnitude of his offense, fearful of the punishment he will have to suffer in the next life, and doubtful about the possibility of God's forgiveness. He almost wholly overlooks the girl's predicament and concerns himself with the need for repentance and "getting back to God." The other student, though aware of the religious significance of his actions, worries most about what he has done to the girl and what the pregnancy might do to her future. Because of this concern he is determined to marry her, even though he neither loves her nor thinks that the marriage will prove successful. His view of religion emphasizes brotherly love rather than a relationship with God. Here we have an example of two different religious frames of reference that produce two divergent reactions to a similar experience. To understand the students the counselor must grasp their fundamental religious views and attitudes.

Understanding

Up to this point, we have stressed the counselor's need to understand as well as he can the counselee's phenomenal field and frame of reference. It remains to indicate why meeting this need is so important. First of all, as we have previously stated, understanding is an essential element in any kind of counseling. An individual feels understood when he experiences a certain kinship with another. He may express it in this way: "Father Smith knows what I am talking about; my wife does not." What he means is that Father Smith somehow grasps how he thinks and feels about the matter under discussion. For a time Father Smith has put aside his own thoughts on the matter in order to concentrate on what the counselee's words mean to the counselee. When the counselee talks to his wife, she is so concerned about her own involvement that she does not make an effort to see things the way he does.

A second reason why it is important for the counselor to understand the counselee's point of view is that this understanding helps the counselee to relax and look at aspects of the problem that have not previously occurred to him. He widens his perceptual field and becomes more rational, since what he sees is less distorted by emotion. He permits the counselor to discuss matters that were previously too disturbing. He begins to sort out the important from the unimportant and to see the essential elements and details in their proper perspective. Gradually he becomes better able to grasp the situation as it actually is rather than as he would like it to be.

When this occurs he is in a better position to make a decision and to act.

A third consequence of the counselor's efforts to understand the counselee's frame of reference is a change that takes place within the counselor. He attains a better grasp of the problem under discussion and can offer sound suggestions, if the situation should call for a more direct approach. His suggestions will make more sense to the counselee, because they will fit into his picture of things.

In this chapter we have described several aspects of the counselee's inner world, pointing out that the counselor needs to understand what is being said from the counselee's point of view as well as from his own. We have analyzed the effects of the phenomenal field and frame of reference. We shall next consider two major influences on the counselee's view of the world, threat and defense reactions.

References

[1] C. R. Rogers, "A Theory of Therapy, Personality and Interpersonal Relationships as Developed in a Client-Centered Framework," in *Psychology: A Study of a Science* (Vol. 3), ed. S. Koch (New York: McGraw-Hill Book Company, 1959), pp. 212–19.

[2] *Ibid*, pp. 265–68.

[3] Rogers does not clearly distinguish the perceptual field from the phenomenal. The above discussion attempts to distinguish the two. Cf. *Client-Centered Therapy* (Boston: Houghton Mifflin Company, 1951), pp. 483–86.

[4] Rogers, *Client-Centered Therapy*, pp. 483–524.

[5] A. W. Combs and Donald Snygg, *Individual Behavior* (New York: Harper & Row, Publishers, 1959), pp. 16–22.

[6] Rogers, *Client-Centered Therapy*, p. 483.

[7] Combs and Snygg, *op. cit.*, p. 20.

[8] James E. Coleman, *Personality Dynamics and Effective Behavior* (Chicago: Scott & Foresman & Company, 1960), pp. 291–315.

[9] Coleman, *op. cit.*, pp. 61–72.

[10] Erik H. Erikson, *Childhood and Society* (New York: W. W. Norton & Company, Inc., 1950).

[11] Rogers, "A Theory of Therapy, Personality and Interpersonal Relationships," pp. 262–63.

[12] Sidney M. Jourard, *Personal Adjustment* (New York: The Macmillan Company, 1963), pp. 170–74.

[13] Combs and Snygg, *op. cit.*, pp. 159–61.

[14] Rogers, "A Theory of Therapy, Personality and Interpersonal Relationships," pp. 265–67.

[15] Combs and Snygg, *op. cit.*, p. 147.

[16] Combs and Snygg, *op. cit.*, pp. 170–80.

[17] C. R. Rogers, "Client-Centered Psychotherapy," *Scientific American*, CLXXXVII, No. 5 (1952), 66–74.

8

The Experience
of Threat
and Coping Devices

Most people who seek religious counseling feel a certain ambivalence. They want assistance but they are reluctant to take the risks that counseling may demand. In their minds counseling has some mystery surrounding it. It is not easy for an individual to open himself to another person and talk about himself and his problems. For this reason, people generally look upon counseling as a threat, even though they foresee that they will benefit from the experience. Moreover, the individual who comes for counseling cannot be sure how he will be received. Perhaps he has heard of another person who sought help from a religious counselor and met with moralizing or even outright rejection. As a consequence he may hesitate to get involved, at least during the initial phase of the contact.

In an effort to ward off potential danger some counselees spend the first part of the session testing the counselor to determine where they stand. Others decide before they begin the counseling to limit their remarks to less personal matters. They are willing to talk about a husband or wife but not about themselves. They are willing to discuss a problem but not their involvement in the problem, to place the blame on another person but not on themselves. Each of us tenaciously protects his self-concept. We each have a definite view of our abilities, talents, and qualifications and are loath to relinquish even the smallest part of this view.[1] Strange as it may seem, we may cling just as strongly to our convictions of deficiencies as to our convictions of assets. Anything which contradicts our view of ourselves poses a threat. We protect the self-concept with the same ferocity that we protect our physical lives. To a degree, therefore, all counseling presents a threat.

Religious Counseling as a Threat

In some respects, religious counseling is more threatening than other forms of counseling. The religious counselor is committed to a code of conduct based on Christian principles. The ultimate reason why he is engaged in counseling is to further the Christian way of life. It is sometimes part of his duty to pass judgment on people's actions. He urges the good to be better and the sinful to mend their ways. In the pulpit his words are frequently judgmental; most people expect that he will pursue the same course in the rectory parlor. Thus the traditional role of the religious counselor as a clergyman makes his task more difficult than that of the vocational or psychological counselor. A judgment generally involves a threat to one's self-concept.[2] To be judged guilty of wrongdoing in any form or to be deprecated undermines self-esteem. Some people equate sinfulness with worthlessness. It is important, therefore, for the religious counselor to realize that he presents a threat, even though those who come for help may appear externally docile and eager to accept whatever he has to say. An essential part of effective counseling is removing as much of the threat as possible so that the counselee can be open and trusting.

Besides the threat presented by the counseling situation, the counselee often faces the added threat posed by the problem which prompted him to come. A person who is at odds with a spouse or teen-aged son or who is wrestling with doubts about faith feels that the situation threatens his self-concept. He recognizes the possibility that some limitation within himself is causing the trouble. Any counseling situation forces the person to confront and to take stock of himself, though he may use a variety of devices to avoid doing it. This fear of self-confrontation often makes the counselee hesitant and uneasy in the initial phases of counseling.

Restriction of
the Perceptual Field

One of the first effects of threat is a restriction of the perceptual field.[3] The individual is fully absorbed by the disturbing problem, and the rest of the world fades into the background. Frequently the individual is able to see not the whole situation but just the menacing part of it. At the moment the only thing of any importance is the dilemma or conflict. Psychologists sometimes call this phenomenon "tunnel vision" because of the effect the threatening circumstances have upon the perceptual field.[4] It is like looking at something through a tunnel or a tube; what is at the end of the tube can be seen clearly but the surrounding area is blocked from vision. Many individuals who enter the counselor's office experience "tunnel vision." They are so taken up with the distressing aspects of the situation that they are unable to look beyond to the extenuating circumstances. No matter how much effort and patience is exercised in an attempt to widen their perceptual field, these counselees sometimes cling to a limited and inaccurate view. At the time they cannot afford to consider all the possibilities. They are afraid that what they might see would harm their self-concept and self-esteem.[5] This is one of the reasons why giving advice at such a time is frequently ineffective. As we stated before, most religious counselors have had the experience of offering what they considered sound advice, only to have it fall on deaf ears. Either the counselee openly rejected what they said and argued against it, or while politely affirming the wisdom of the advice rejected it inwardly. In such instances, the advice is simply outside of the counselee's perceptual field and it makes no sense to him. A pastor may offer a hysterical mother many suggestions about ways to handle a rebellious teen-aged daughter who has taken to smoking marijuana, but probably the advice will be of little avail until the woman can look upon the problem in a calmer and more reasonable way. For the present, the whole situation is too threatening; she cannot apply what the counselor says to her personal situation. It is true that she hears his words and may even be able to repeat them to a neighbor, but they have little meaning for her. She does not regard them as an answer to her difficulty, even though they may well provide the answer.

The "Safe" Approach

Still another protection against threat is the "safe" approach.[6] Under stress an individual's security is frequently undermined, especially if he is an insecure person to start with. Under attack a person is no longer so sure of himself as formerly. He begins to doubt his capabilities and loses some of his confidence. As a consequence he is no longer willing to risk the possibility of failure. He relies on proven methods of handling situations and rejects new, unproven ones. If he hears novel advice he immediately puts it aside as too dangerous. During counseling sessions people often resort to the "safe" approach. The obviously-shaken counselee is unable to accept advice because following through on it is too risky— at least at the present time. Were he to do what was suggested, his wife might actually divorce him or his son might actually get in trouble with the law. At the moment he is too insecure to tolerate even the possibility of such an outcome; he retreats to the safe method of appeasement, which though perhaps futile is at least familiar and tried. When the immediate threat subsides, the counselee can often widen his perceptual field and break away from the "safe" approach. He can then look at the matter more objectively and come up with other ways of handling it.

Personality and Threat

People faced with threatening situations differ considerably in their reactions. Some stand up to their problems and decide upon adequate means of coping with them; others deny that the situation really threatens them; and still others distort the situation so that it no longer appears to be a threat. To understand the counselee's attitudes, one needs to know something about his coping techniques.

The individual with a well-balanced personality usually confronts a problem directly. First of all, he admits that the situation is threatening to him. He sees that it attacks his opinions or even his person. He makes no attempt to hide his anxiety. Furthermore, when he seeks counseling he knows that at first he will not be completely at ease. He accepts this state of mind and may even begin the discussion by saying exactly how he feels. His anxiety, however, does not become so great that it keeps him from evaluating the situation accurately. He is able to bring everything out into the open. Once he has done this he can examine the various ways of handling the matter and settle on the one that seems best for the time being. He then resolves to modify his behavior in accordance with this decision and the counseling session is successfully concluded.

Unfortunately many people who seek religious counseling do not possess completely healthy personalities. Some lack inner strength and cannot stand up to stressful situations; they must use subterfuges like denial. In this case the counselee may begin with such words as "I don't know why I am bothering you. What I want to talk about really is not very important, but I thought I ought to drop by anyway." In effect he is trying to say that the matter is very important but at present too threatening to face. A direct confrontation would evoke too much anxiety; he finds it easier to side-step the issue. He convinces himself that it is not important to him. A second counselee might handle a similar problem in quite a different fashion. He might begin by saying, "My wife is very upset about this matter, but I don't think things are as bad as she makes them out to be. I really think she is the one who should be talking with you." In this instance the counselee admits that there is a problem, but he denies that it refers to him and instead attributes it to another person. His way of handling the anxiety is to use his wife as a distractor. Finally, a counselee might use delaying tactics. He is perhaps not yet ready to confront the issues. He may even be open enough to admit it, saying: "I don't have to come to any decision right now, but I thought it might be well to discuss it with someone." His initial intent in seeking counseling is not to arrive at some definite conclusions but simply to have the opportunity to unburden himself. This individual realizes indirectly that at present he is too anxious and concerned to arrive at a reasonable solution. Naturally, if the counselor pushes for a solution, he meets with immediate resistance.

Defense Reactions

The human mind has many ways of escaping the intolerable. One of Freud's major contributions to understanding human nature is his treatise on defense mechanisms.[7] Somewhat later Dollard and Miller subjected this theory to rigorous research and placed it on a more solid foundation.[8] When an individual is unable to face either internal or external stress, he may resort to defensive tactics.[9] We have just examined one such tactic, denial, and there are many others. The particular defense tactic that a person uses is the product of experience and learning. Frequent repetition makes it a habitual response, part of the usual repertoire of responses. Each time a person uses a defense he lessens his anxiety—usually unknown to himself—and as a result, he comes to rely more and more on that reaction.

As small children we learn that a direct confrontation with parental authority leads to frustration, anxiety, guilt, and punishment; yet we still want to have our own way. We learn devious ways of coping with this distressing situation. Frequently these coping techniques are quite similar to those used by our parents. The child who hears his mother wiggle out of a detested parent-teachers' committee meeting on the grounds of a terrible headache may soon use the same excuse when faced with a test at school. And strangely enough the boy really may have a headache. Repetition makes the excuse as routine as tying his shoes. Although each time a person uses a defense mechanism he lessens anxiety and tension, no defense is fully effective.[10] In some instances part of the anxiety lingers in the back of the mind. Sometimes the defense brings on new stress, even though it does eliminate the immediate threat. The boy who develops headaches to avoid examinations—and often he is not aware of why he gets the headache—soon discovers that he is failing in school, and he is subjected to new pressures both at home and at school. Other defenses, as we shall presently see, interfere with effective living. A further limitation of defensive coping devices is the exorbitant amount of energy they require. Even though the individual is often not aware of the price he is paying to lessen anxiety and fear, the maintenance of an extensive defense system saps much of the energy that could be used in more constructive pursuits.

Need for Defenses

The above discussion should not lead to the conclusion that all defensive tactics are harmful.[11] Some are quite necessary to our psychological equilibrium. Were we suddenly to be stripped of our defenses, we might have a mental breakdown. This possibility is especially strong for inadequate personalities. At times it is healthy to side-step an issue for awhile; to meet it head-on would only bring disaster. In such instances a person's defense reactions can protect him from lasting damage.

In attempting to understand the counselee's inner world, the religious counselor should recognize his unique coping systems. Such recognition is necessary not to persuade the individual to abandon his debilitating defenses, but rather to communicate a sense of understanding to him. The counselor shows that he can comprehend why the counselee uses certain defense mechanisms. This understanding may bring the whole problem into the open, where the counselee can examine it without being afraid that he will be condemned for being irrational or foolish.

In dealing with defense mechanisms, it is not so much the particular tactic that is important but rather the problem that underlies it. Sometimes in an atmosphere of understanding an individual can first realize that he is using a particular defense and then perhaps discover what lies behind it. The purpose of religious counseling, however, is not to bring about this kind of personality change. Such change might occur, but the counselor does not make it one of his goals. If he is to understand the counselee and his problem, however, he should recognize the effect that defenses have on the problem itself and on the counseling.

We have already considered examples of a basic defense mechanism, denial. By denying that a problem exists, the individual avoids the anxiety that the difficulty might provoke.[12] A somewhat similar device is repression.[13] In this defense the person unconsciously blocks from his awareness certain feelings and impulses. Thus, he may be very angry about his wife's belittling attitude, but he experiences only a feeling of indifference. Although repression is one of the most frequently used defenses, its manifestations are so subtle that they often require analysis by a trained person.

Examples of Defense Reactions

During the course of a working day, the religious counselor meets many types of defense mechanisms. Let us consider some of the more obvious examples.

A father whose teen-age son has become involved with the juvenile authorities because of repeated truancy and auto theft comes to his pastor for advice. He is obviously shaken by the incident. At one point in the discussion, he says, "I have been so busy with my work that I really have not given the boy the time I should have." If the father were honest with himself, he would admit that he is using a defensive tactic to avoid facing the possibility that he has failed as a parent. The tactic that he is using is called rationalization.[14] If he had a genuine fatherly interest in the son, he would have arranged his work schedule to have sufficient time for him. Since admitting this would be too devastating to his self-concept, he resorts to rationalization. No one likes to admit failure in one of his main obligations in life.

Another common defense is projection.[15] A forty-year-old, overly pious, unmarried woman comes in to discuss her deteriorating personal relationships. She is convinced that most of the women in the office where she works are talking about her. She thinks that they hate her because they are jealous over special favors she has received from her employer. As the interview progresses, it becomes clear that the woman has only vague and inconsistent evidence for her convictions. She is a physically unattractive person with a bland personality. In many respects she has rejected herself, but she resorts to projection to avoid admitting this to herself. She blocks the reality of her self-hatred from consciousness and instead attributes this feeling to other people, affirming that the women in the office hate her and are spreading malicious lies about her. To justify her position she imagines that her fellow workers experience jealousy over special favors she has received from her employer. This psychological device allows her to live with herself by protecting an already limited self-concept.

One type of repression is called emotional insulation.[16] A haggard-looking mother of six small children comes to the rectory with the two youngest, one of whom is obviously sick. Her manner of speaking and acting is vivacious. After a few pleasantries, she launches into the heart of the matter, her problems with an alcoholic husband who is unable to support his many children. At the conclusion of a depressing account of poverty and struggle, she remarks, "My husband's drinking really doesn't bother me. I am just concerned about his spiritual welfare because I love him very much." She has found that the only way she can live is by refusing to allow her true feelings to become conscious. She denies that she feels any concern or anxiety. She has a sick child and no medication, six children and no food, but she thinks that somehow she will manage. She does not allow herself to experience anger toward her husband or toward her depressing situation. She does not permit her fears or love for her sick child to come to the surface. As a consequence, she does not face the basic problems or take steps to improve her condition.

Another defensive reaction can be seen in the mother of several children who becomes absorbed in every possible parish or school activity. She makes herself always available, thereby delighting the pastor and his assistants. She seems to play a prominent role in almost every function. Psychologists call her defense a flight into activity.[17] As long as her attention is directed toward many projects, she does not have time to be bothered by marital discord or feelings of inadequacy as a parent. Her self-esteem is enhanced by success in parish and school activities. Most people, including the pastor, consider her an outstanding leader and a paragon of normality, but in reality she is escaping inner turmoil through social activity.

Within the same parish she may have a counterpart who has solved her inner problems by dedicating herself to personal "holiness." This individual attends all the novenas, rosaries, and miscellaneous church ceremonies. The purpose of the "holy" activity is to divert attention from a real inner problem, such as loneliness or a feeling of rejection. As long as most of her life is taken up with prayer, there is no time to worry about anything else. Furthermore, being "holy" does enhance her view of herself. Of course, not everyone who engages in parish activities or religious ceremonies is motivated by unconscious defenses, but the religious counselor should realize that such motivation is at work in some instances.

A final example is the individual who, because of his defense mechanisms, never comes to the counselor's office at all. He uses isolation as a means of protecting his self-concept.[18] He finds withdrawing from reality the most convenient coping device. He can no longer battle the world, so he retreats to the safety of his home and rarely ventures out. He engages in extended day-dreaming, hours of TV-watching, or endless novel-reading. From experience he has found that he is no longer able to cope with everyday life. Rather than face failure, he builds a more tolerable world within his imagination or engages in some kind of vicarious experience. It is usually a distraught parent or relative who comes to the counselor, seeking advice about how to handle such an individual. If the counselor is to be helpful, it is important that he understand what underlies this choice of defense.

Reducing Threat

One of the first tasks in any form of counseling is to create a psychological atmosphere that lessens the experience of threat. As long as the counselee is suffering from the consequences of threat and anxiety, he will remain highly defensive and will be unable to look at himself and his problems in their true perspective. Counseling tries to make the counselee feel more secure and sure of himself so that he will be more open to reality. The more facts that he can accurately perceive and evaluate, the better are his chances of finding an effective answer. If his view is distorted or limited to a small, disturbing aspect of the situation, he will overlook many circumstances that are important for a correct evaluation. One common distortion is to magnify possible consequences of the difficulty beyond reasonable proportions. In this case the counselee needs the opportunity to talk freely and openly without fear of being judged or deprecated for having a problem. The counselor must be careful that his attitude or manner does not make the counselee feel threatened.

The religious counselor, like any other counselor, must handle the experience of threat and establish an atmosphere which will allow the counselee to see his real self. Effective counseling begins when the counselee can say "I do know" or "I can face it" or "It is I" (and not someone else).[19] In some ways the religious counselor has a more difficult assignment than his fellow counselors. His role as a clergyman or dedicated person sets him on a pedestal; he is looked upon as an exemplary person with high ideals and values. The counselee's feeling that he cannot live up to the expectations of such a person may deplete his self-esteem. The religious counselor is therefore forced to make a considerable effort to create a nonthreatening atmosphere. There are certain procedures he should avoid and others that he should utilize. Perhaps the most important thing to avoid is any mannerism or expression that would indicate an attitude of superiority. If he gives the impression that he has all the answers because of his superior education, he immediately belittles the counselee and makes him feel inferior, with the result that the counselee strengthens his defenses to protect what self-esteem he has left. If the counselor's superior attitude is pronounced, he may accomplish nothing more than to make the counselee more defensive than ever.

Judgment and Defense Reactions

From early childhood people have passed judgments on our actions. Negative judgments often put us on the defensive.[20] When six-year-old Johnny tears his new pants while skating, his mother greets him with "You are a bad boy; you tore your pants." Johnny immediately retorts "I am not. I didn't do it. Jimmy pushed me." Mother has made a negative judgment which has weakened Johnny's self-esteem. Johnny has reacted by putting up his defenses. Many adults have not changed their defensive reactions essentially from the time when they were children, except for finding more subtle and complex ways of defending themselves. If the counselor assumes the role of a parent and passes judgment, he may very well hear the same kind of response that Johnny's mother did. Judgmental statements should have a limited use in religious counseling. Circumstances may occasionally arise which call for such statements, since the religious counselor is looked upon also as a teacher of Christian morality and will sometimes be asked whether a particular action is right or wrong; but he should use this procedure as seldom as possible.

Most people who have relatively stable personalities either understand the moral implications of their actions already or, if given some basic principles, can easily draw their own conclusions. The parish alcoholic or the teen-age Don Juan knows that what he is doing does not conform with Christian principles of living. He does not need someone to tell him that he is doing wrong. Dwelling on the sinfulness of these actions only causes greater guilt and defensiveness.

It hardly seems necessary to point out that there is almost never an occasion for "hell and damnation" exhortations in religious counseling, except perhaps as a last resort in the case of the psychopath who has lost all sense of guilt and shame. If there is a need for such a procedure, it is certainly not in the initial phases of counseling. At the start of the session the counselee is usually uneasy, anxious, and threatened. The "hell and damnation" approach can only serve to heighten this tension radically. In some instances it may even serve to throw the counselee into a state of panic with grave spiritual and psychological consequences.

To lessen the experience of threat and make the individual open to the various aspects of his problem, the counselor must demonstrate a genuinely accepting, friendly attitude.[21] This attitude includes, first of all, a deep respect for the worth of the counselee. Counselors with seminary training may have a tendency to put the person of the counselee in the background and make the ramifications of the abstract problem all-important. They may regard the counselee not as a person but as an object with a problem, perhaps one of the many typical problems described in a text on moral theology or pastoral psychology. Effective counseling demands a real interest in the counselee as an individual. If the counselor is unable to take an interest in a particular counselee, he will have difficulty achieving any lasting results. If the religious counselor does not particularly like dealing with people or likes only some people, he should not attempt counseling or should limit his counseling to those whom he can meet without antipathy.

Showing Interest in the Counselee

The counselor shows interest in the counselee by genuinely listening to him and trying to understand things from his point of view. He wants to listen not because of some personal need or gain but rather because of a real liking for the counselee. This liking may be based on Christian charity and brotherhood or simply on the attractive personal characteristics of a particular counselee. Naturally, the degree of liking and interest will fluctuate. Since all counselors are human, there will be occasions when a counselor will have to give counsel without being in the mood for such an activity, but his general attitude is nevertheless one of acceptance and understanding. If this attitude is genuine, the counselee will recognize spontaneously the almost imperceptible proofs of interest and concern.

One might ask how being interested in another person helps him solve a personal problem, whether one of spiritual development or one of family relations. First of all, genuine interest and respect make the individual feel that he is a worthwhile, mature person capable of dealing with the ordinary problems of daily living. If he is treated like a child, he will be convinced that he really is a child incapable of facing life-problems. Secondly, the fact that another person thinks enough of what he has to say to devote his undivided attention to it indicates to the counselee that his thoughts and observation must have some value and are worthy of consideration. The counselor's confidence in the counselee builds up the counselee's confidence in himself; as a consequence he feels more secure in examining even the most threatening aspects of his problem. He is then in a position to consider every ramification of the problem and eventually reach a solution on his own. And finally, the opportunity to reveal his inner feelings and experiences is therapeutic in itself; it also helps to get the matter out in the open where it can be evaluated objectively.[22]

References

[1]Arthur W. Combs and Donald Snygg, *Individual Behavior* (New York: Harper & Row, Publishers, 1959), p. 130.

[2] Carl R. Rogers, *On Becoming a Person* (Boston: Houghton Mifflin, 1961), pp. 54–55.

[3] Combs and Snygg, *op. cit.*, pp. 170–72.

[4] *Ibid.*, p. 167.

[5] *Ibid.*, p. 146.

6 *Ibid.,* pp. 188–89.

7 Sigmund Freud, *The Problem of Anxiety* (New York: W. W. Norton & Company, Inc., 1936).

8 John Dollard and Neal E. Miller, *Personality and Psychotherapy* (New York: McGraw-Hill Book Company, 1950).

9 Otto Fenichel, *The Psychoanalytic Theory of Neurosis* (New York: W. W. Norton & Company, Inc., 1945), pp. 130–40.

10 James C. Coleman, *Personality Dynamics and Effective Behavior* (Chicago: Scott, Foresman & Company, 1960), pp. 196–207.

11 A. A. Schneiders, *Personality Dynamics and Mental Health* (New York: Holt, Rinehart and Winston, Inc., 1965), p. 250.

12 Anna Freud, *The Ego and Mechanisms of Defence* (London: The Hogarth Press, 1937).

13 Sigmund Freud, *A General Introduction to Psychoanalysis* (New York: Washington Square Press, 1960), pp. 297–311.

14 Schneiders, *op. cit.,* pp. 244–45.

15 *Ibid.,* pp. 248–49; Fenichel, *op. cit.,* pp. 146–47.

16 Coleman, *op. cit.,* pp. 203–4.

17 Schneiders, *op. cit.,* p. 219.

18 *Ibid.,* pp. 285–90.

19 Seward Hiltner, "Clinical and Theological Notes on Responsibility," *Journal of Religion and Health,* II (1962) 7–20.

20 Rogers, *op. cit.,* p. 54.

21 Carl R. Rogers, *Client-Centered Therapy* (Boston: Houghton Mifflin Company, 1951), pp. 19–64.

22 Sidney M. Jourard, *The Transparent Self* (New York: D. Van Nostrand Co., Inc., 1964), pp. 9–16.

9

Feelings and Emotions

Feelings and emotions play an important but often unnoticed role in the average person's daily life. An employee with
six children makes an error in judgment which costs the firm several thousand dollars. He is reprehended and told that a similar
mistake will mean the end of his job. As a result he begins to experience guilt and fear which make him feel less confident on the
job and edgy, restless, and ill-at-ease at home. His friends notice
that he is quieter and more reserved. Detecting a change in himself, particularly in his relationship with his wife, he may approach
his pastor for counseling. He may be vague about his reason for
coming and may latch on to something inconsequential, like a disagreement with his wife over the disciplining of their children or
the provisions for their religious education. The source of the
trouble, however, lies in his inability to recognize how thoroughly
his life is being disrupted by the emotions of guilt and fear.

Most of us recognize emotional experience, but when we are
asked to define what it means we may be at a loss.[1] We have all
felt happy or sad; we have shared love and joy with others; we
have become angry or fearful. These are all common inner experiences which color our contacts with people and things. Allport
has defined emotions as "stirred up conditions of the organism." [2]
They act as instigators, helping us get what we need to survive and

grow as people. At times they are danger signals telling us that something is wrong and that we had better alter our course of action. They constitute that part of mental functioning which psychologists call *affective*. The affect refers to feelings and emotions as opposed to reason and will.[3] Because traditional theology places the emphasis on knowledge and responsibility, the affective side of mental life is likely to be overlooked.

Feelings

Affective reactions are frequently separated into two types, feelings and emotions. Feelings can be defined as positive or negative reactions to an experience.[4] They usually result from something that we like or dislike, and they are less intense than emotions such as fear, anger, or jealousy. When one has a positive affective reaction, he experiences pleasure. For example, at breakfast a man may find a cup of hot coffee pleasant but while waiting for his wife to fix it, he experiences a negative, unpleasant reaction.[5]

Emotions

Emotions are more profound, pervasive, and intense than feelings.[6] There is, however, no sharp line of demarcation between these two states. One distinction between them is that an emotion is usually attached to a definite object or class of objects. The individual is afraid of dogs or rooms with high ceilings. He is angry at his wife or his employer. These objects actually cause his emotion, though he may be unaware of the connection.

To grasp the counselee's frame of reference, it is necessary to understand his affective reactions; such understanding requires some knowledge of how feelings and emotions work. One of the more obvious emotional qualities is spontaneity.[7] In a terrifying situation the individual automatically experiences fear. The soldier who is pinned down in a cross-fire is afraid, though he may try to repress or rationalize away his fear. He appraises the extreme danger in which he finds himself and immediately undergoes an emotional response. He can control his actions, but he cannot turn off the emotional reaction. A common misconception is that the man of character has complete control over his emotions and can turn them on and off at will. Actually fear, anger, jealousy, and guilt are spontaneous reactions which cannot be controlled by the will, once the individual has become aware of the object which stimulates them. Hence the individual is not responsible for such emotions. The guilt-ridden counselee does not choose to feel guilty, nor can he free himself from guilt through an act of will. He will continue to experience guilt until he comes to terms with its causes through such measures as confession. He can control the sinful act but not the affective response.

Function of Fear and Guilt

Emotions like fear, anger, and guilt can be either helpful or harmful. Since the experience of guilt is painful, the desire to avoid it often motivates the individual to follow his moral code; if the temptation is too strong and he does violate the code, his guilt may prompt sorrow, amendment, and reparation. When guilt feelings are not relieved they continue to build up and can lead to "acting out," as in the case of an alcoholic who continues his compulsive drinking to escape his guilt; in other cases they may lead to a period of depression.

Guilt is similar to fear in many ways. We might even call it moral fear. Fear is often an extremely useful experience, as it warns us to stay away from danger. If we were completely fearless, we would have trouble staying alive. Virtually every emotion can, under certain circumstances, have a beneficial effect, if it prompts us to protect or develop ourselves either physically or psychologically.

The Appraisal

An emotional response involves an appraisal.[8] A person who is afraid of snakes appraises them as potentially dangerous. When he sees a snake in a field, he automatically evaluates it as a thing to be avoided. Many of our emotions are learned from either personal experience or contact with others. The man who has been bitten learns to fear snakes as a result of his unfortunate experience.

The child feels guilty for stealing his friend's baseball because he has been taught that stealing is wrong. Since each individual has a different set of learning experiences, his emotional reactions are unique.[9] The counselor should grasp as best he can the nature of the counselee's emotional experience. Emotional responses form an important part of the counselee's frame of reference. Thus, one boy may be overcome with guilt and shame once he realizes he is guilty of stealing, whereas another child may shrug off his deed as inconsequential. In helping either child, the counselor should concentrate on the particular emotional reaction.

There is a correlation between emotion and intelligence. A brighter person tends to have a more complex emotional life, and thus he is more difficult to understand. "This fact suggests that emotional disturbance is like a temporary breakdown in a piece of machinery or electrical equipment; the more complex the equipment, the greater number of things by which the operation may be disturbed, the greater the aberration from normal function may be and the longer it may take to get it back in working order." [10]

Emotions follow a developmental sequence like any other component of the human organism.[11] As the child grows, his body develops and takes on more mature contours; similarly, his emotions take on more mature patterns of expression. The emotional reactions of a small child are shortlived; those of the adolescent and adult are more prolonged.[12] The frequent outbursts of the small child may appear quite violent but are actually shallow. A trivial frustration may evoke a tantrum, but five minutes later the child has forgotten the incident. An adult's response lasts longer and usually requires a more significant cause. Emotional immaturity is a failure on the part of an adolescent or an adult to outgrow some of his childish emotional patterns. He is still having certain reactions of anger or fear which were a part of his affective repertoire when he was four or five years old. For example, he becomes excessively angry when contradicted and responds with a childish outburst. In happy circumstances he is momentarily overcome with euphoria, but his experience has little depth or duration. Maturity level is an important part of the frame of reference and must be taken into consideration in counseling. If the counselor presumes that all counselees experience the same emotional reactions as he does, he will make the counselee feel misunderstood.

Handling Emotions

An emotional experience can be handled in several different ways. It can be expressed openly, channeled, suppressed, or repressed.[13] Some people develop the habit of constantly expressing their emotions. They "wear their hearts on their sleeves." They are effusive and demonstrative. Other people do not seem to have an emotion in their bodies. They may be experiencing the same emotions as the first group, but they do not show their feelings. Both types of response have their limitations. The individual who constantly expresses his feelings may often find himself at odds with his society. Flying off the handle or bursting into tears is unacceptable behavior in most cultures. Rage, a violent form of anger accompanied by threatened or actual attack, elicits either disapproval or a similar rage—and perhaps a fight—from the other person.

When we are unable to express our emotions or think it unwise to do so, we can either channel or inhibit them. Channeling involves acknowledging our emotions and choosing some indirect means of expression. For instance, a man becomes angry with his wife but instead of attacking her either verbally or physically, he goes outside and plays a game of touch football with his sons. In this way he channels his pent-up anger constructively by running up and down the field and blocking an opponent. He works off his anger and at the same time contributes to a better relationship with his sons.

There are occasions, however, when we can neither express nor channel our emotions and must either suppress or repress them. Suppression implies a voluntary attempt to put aside the emotion, repression an involuntary blocking of the emotion from consciousness. In suppression, the individual determines that he is going to stop thinking angry thoughts. Each time hateful thoughts return to his mind, he actively tries to banish them. In the case of repression, the individual does not even know that he is angry or at least does not realize how angry he is. He may feel vaguely uncomfortable, but he does not realize why he is experiencing the hostility. Of all the methods of handling feelings and emotions, repression can be the most destructive. Repressed feelings are dangerous to both physical and psychological equilibrium. Sometimes anger may suddenly crop up in an unfounded attack on a bystander, and the angry person will be at a loss to explain his actions. A most important requisite in coping with one's emotions is to acknowledge and accept them. Once a person acknowledges to himself that he is angry at a particular individual or situation, he can begin to control his actions. If he experiences only a vague feeling of frustration and hostility, he cannot cope with himself or the situation. Sometimes by talking things over with another person, like a counselor, he can see how he really feels and can deal with the cause of his emotion.

Feelings and Motivation

A major effect of feelings and emotions is motivation.[14] Frequently we do something because it is pleasant or refuse to do something else because it is unpleasant. Our feelings provide the driving force behind our activity. Without our feelings and emotions we would probably become stagnant. We would have little incentive to undertake the difficult or to avoid the harmful. Often the main cause of a person seeking counseling is emotional. He feels anxious about the deterioration of his marriage; he is depressed about the lack of meaning in his life; or he is angry about the recent innovations in the church and has considered abandoning his faith. It is unlikely that intellectual convictions alone would make him seek help from a counselor; his distressing emotions provide the strongest impetus. This distress usually also motivates the severely neurotic person to begin psychotherapy or counseling and to continue through many painful hours of therapy to completion. We all find it difficult to live with distressing emotions like fear, anger, jealousy, or anxiety, and we all look for means of escape. The counselor and the psychiatrist utilize this human characteristic in their dealings with individuals.

Emotional Abreaction

One function of counseling is to effect an abreaction. This term signifies a release or weakening of emotional tensions caused by conflict or repression.[15] In the nonthreatening counseling atmosphere, the counselee is able to speak freely about how he feels.

Talking about his anger or fears can lessen his distress and make him more relaxed. In some instances, the religious counselor's main purpose is to cause an emotional abreaction. Actually, the expression of anger does not necessarily exhaust it. Sometimes talking about a situation makes the counselee grow even angrier. It is necessary not only to discuss feelings and emotions but also to appraise the source and circumstances of the reactions.[16] When the counselee can see that there are other, better responses to the situation, he can usually put aside his anger. Better control and greater ability to make rational decisions often result from the abreaction.[17]

Common Affective Reactions in Counseling

There are four affective reactions that are most frequently encountered in religious counseling: anxiety, hostility, guilt, and grief. Anxiety is a part of every man's life. It can be described more accurately as a feeling than as an emotion. It ranges from a mild motivating force to a severely painful experience. Anxiety is a state of apprehension, concern and uneasiness, closely related to fear. It is distinguished from fear primarily by its vagueness and lack of a definite object.[18] When the counselee is anxious, he is concerned about an undefined future danger. He is apprehensive that something may happen, but he is not sure what.[19] This unpleasant state of mind frequently prompts someone to seek an escape or to seek help from a counselor.

Anxiety is often accompanied by worry. The anxious person wonders, "What is going to happen to me?" and worries, "What will I do when . . . ?" A counselor need not be in business very long before he comes across a person who is worried about a multitude of things, some significant and others inconsequential. He is apprehensive about his wife's health (which actually is average for a woman of forty-five), his job (where he has received a raise every year for the past five years), the loss of a friend (who was not a close friend anyway), arriving late for an appointment, and a host of other concerns expressed during a single half hour. Such an individual is probably experiencing a high level of anxiety, which he attaches to almost any convenient object. To understand this counselee's frame of reference it is necessary to keep in mind that he is a highly anxious person who really does not know what is causing his anxiety.

Anxiety, like any other affective response, can be beneficial as well as destructive. An experienced preacher often knows that he is most effective when he feels somewhat anxious. A mild level of anxiety sharpens one's capabilities and leads to a better performance. Even daily living brings a certain amount of anxiety.[20] We are all vaguely apprehensive about the possibility of an accident, a war, or personal failure. Only when anxiety exceeds the normal level does it become a handicap.

"Normal anxiety is proportionate to the objective danger and is relieved when the threat is removed, while neurotic anxiety is enduring and disproportionate." [21] Neurotic anxiety can become so extreme it disrupts normal functioning. The neurotic individual may find that his thinking, reasoning, and concentration are impaired. He may be restless and irritable and may even reach the stage when he feels as if he is "falling apart." Obviously such a person needs more intensive care than the religious counselor can provide.

Hostility and Anger

Hostility is a second affective reaction that enters into religious counseling. Like anxiety it is vague and can be better described as a feeling than as an emotion. It is not so easy to perceive as anxiety, since many of its manifestations are disguised. Hostility is a vague expression of anger in the form of sarcastic, belittling, hypercritical, or nagging remarks.[22] Often neither the counselor nor the counselee realizes the extent of the counselee's hostility and its effect on his capacity to deal with his problems.

Hostility is often the result of frustration and dissatisfaction with one's life.[23] An individual who does not get what he thinks he should from life may become angry without being conscious of the full impact of his anger. Instead he has a mild feeling of discontent, frustration, and depression. Often the source of the reaction is discontent with oneself, although hostility can also result from frustration by other people or by external circumstance.

Like other feelings or emotions, hostility and anger have a

constructive purpose. They give us motivation and stamina to accomplish difficult tasks. Only when these feelings go unrecognized do they become disproportionate and hinder normal functioning.

Both anger and hostility may produce a similar reaction in the person toward whom they are directed. Unless the counselor is conscious of the counselee's hostility toward him, he may, in turn, experience hostility toward the counselee. When he sees signs of hostility in the counselee, he should realize that this hostility is probably not directed at him personally but is instead an instance of general hostility directed at him as the most immediate target. If the counselor interprets this emotion as a personal attack on himself, he will probably react with anger and damage his working relationship with the counselee.

Guilt

Since religion is closely tied to morality, the religious counselor frequently faces the emotion of guilt. "The feeling of guilt may be described as a painful emotion, such as a sense of unworthiness relating to the realization of an over-wide discrepancy between one's own conduct and the moral or ethical code one has set up for himself. As such, guilt feelings are especially internal and personal, since they result from self-judgment by internalized standards." [24] Guilt often causes the individual to change his conduct and follow his moral code. Normally guilt feelings can be relieved through a confession to a clergyman or confidant, an effort to repair any damage that results from the misconduct, a willingness to accept forgiveness, and a determination to look to the future rather than the past. One function of a religious counselor is to accept the counselee's confession and help him derive some profit from his past mistakes.

Some counselees are never convinced that the slate is clean. Much of the time they feel mildly guilty, sometimes about minor infractions of their ethical and moral code and at other times for no apparent reason at all. They are plagued with a pathological guilt. The severely scrupulous counselee sees sin wherever he turns and magnifies his transgressions all out of proportion. He experiences a free-floating guilt which makes him miserable much of the time. Often he is a perfectionist, establishing standards of conduct that are totally beyond his reach. Ordinarily such a person requires the help of a psychiatrist or psychologist.

Grief

A final emotion that often comes to the religious counselor's attention is grief. In times of sorrow, many people turn to a priest or minister. They find solace in expressing openly their sadness and depression. Grief is a normal reaction to losing someone or something that is highly valued.[25] It is often complicated by other feelings, such as hostility, guilt, and depression. The wife whose husband has just died is sometimes bothered by the thought that she was not kind enough during his last illness. Besides experiencing guilt, she also feels an introverted anger at herself. Most people are able to work through their grief by crying, by talking with other people, or by merely letting time pass. Finding a concerned listener often hastens the process. The principal task of the counselor in this case is to create a climate of acceptance and understanding. The counselee who feels that he is talking with someone who cares can express his feelings verbally and handle them more easily. Frequently this is all that he needs. With time, the loss is accepted and the individual returns to his usual state of equilibrium.

Occasionally the counselor is asked to talk with a person who is unable to overcome his grief. For example, a woman whose husband died a year ago still spends several hours each week at his grave, seldom visits her friends, and makes no effort to build a new life for herself. She is frequently on the verge of tears and often breaks down when someone mentions her deceased husband. If the usual approaches to religious counseling fail, the counselor can be certain that there are deeper pathological causes for her grief and that psychiatric care is needed.

Obstacles to Understanding

Determining how another person feels is not an easy task. People hide their emotions, especially those which have some social stigma attached: men are not supposed to be afraid; people should not openly display anger; sentimentality is a sign of weakness. We inhibit our emotional reactions and, if questioned about our feelings, deny them or evade the question with a cliché.

Another obstacle to understanding people's feelings and emotions is that people frequently do not realize how they really feel. From early childhood they learn to repress all undesirable feelings. In adulthood the mechanism works automatically to banish from consciousness many affective reactions. A man who has been passed over for promotion will probably deny that he feels angry and will say instead that he is just disappointed. He has learned from childhood that it does not pay to express anger openly. After years of repression, he can no longer recognize that he feels frustrated or angry about the injustice. The counselor who wants to convey his understanding to the counselee must somehow surmount these obstacles, indicating that in spite of them he has grasped the counselee's real feelings.

Cues to Understanding

Understanding the emotions and feelings of another person demands sensitivity and experience.[26] A counselor should recognize several indicators or cues to a person's feelings. One helpful cue can be taken from the individual's own words. If he is frank, he will tell you whether he likes you or dislikes you. Many people, however, are too fearful to express their feelings verbally. They tell you what they think you want to hear. This is just as likely to occur in a religious counseling session as in a cocktail lounge. People also may indicate their emotions by their manner of speech or their gestures. They may not say explicitly that they are angry but show it by their clenched fists and sharp tone of voice. The counselor should be alert to the importance of these signs.

Another cue is the type of emotional reaction associated with a certain situation. When one's car goes into a skid on an icy road, one usually responds with fear or panic. As the counselee describes a verbal argument with his wife, the counselor usually can infer, from his knowledge of how most people feel in such a situation, how the counselee feels. From experience most people learn what is the normal affective reaction to a variety of situations. The counselor draws on his experience in attempting to make himself sensitive to the counselee's feelings.

Finally, the counselor uses his own affective experience to help him understand the counselee's feelings and emotions. If the counselor has an undistorted awareness of his own reaction to certain situations, he will be better able to surmise how the counselee feels in a similar situation. Their reactions may differ in some cases, but usually the counselor can follow the hypothesis that healthy people have similar emotional experiences. This cue and the others discussed above can help the counselor understand the counselee's frame of reference, but they require considerable effort.

Interplay of Emotional Experiences

In counseling there is a constant interplay between the emotional experiences of the counselee and the counselor. Each is reacting affectively in his own way to what is happening in the counseling session. The counselor should be aware of what is taking place both within himself and within the counselee. A failure to do this can lead to a breakdown in the relationship. Let us consider, for example, the case of a hostile counselee who has conflicting feelings toward authority because of his stern, overly demanding father. He comes to the pastor's office, pouring forth critical, sarcastic remarks about the Church. The pastor's spontaneous reaction is to meet hostility with hostility. Unless the pastor quickly sizes up what is really taking place, he may become involved in a verbal exchange and may finally show the counselee the door. In this case the pastor's misunderstanding of the counselee's response leads to a counseling failure. Although the pastor may think that the counselee's feelings are directed at him personally or at the Church which he represents, they actually spring from the repressive authoritarianism of the counselee's father. They are merely transferred to the pastor, who is identified as a figure of authority like the father.[27] Unless the pastor is aware of this transference, he cannot handle the counselee adequately.

Each of us has emotional weak spots, usually as a product of the way we were raised. Some may feel inadequate in intellectual conversations; others may feel rejected by those whom they meet for the first time. The religious counselor is usually no exception; he too takes his weak spots into the counseling session. Unless he is aware of his weaknesses, he may react with hostility to a counselee who attacks him at a vulnerable point. Psychiatrists and clinical psychologists frequently undergo psychotherapy to make themselves aware of their emotional weak spots. Such an intensive remedy may not be necessary for the average religious counselor, but he should become aware of his personality limitations through self-reflection and personal relations with friends.

The religious counselor should realize that it is normal and healthy to express emotions, as long as such expression does not harm himself or other people. There are occasions that call for the expression of anger and fear—though these occasions may cause discomfort to other people and even perhaps to the counselee. The counselor must express his feelings if he wants to be fully human in his dealings with other people. He must learn to accept these emotions for what they are and not resort to repression. He must also learn to accept the counselee's feelings and emotions in the same way, even if they are negative and hostile; only by expressing these feelings will the counselee be able to appraise them accurately, evaluate them objectively, and make any necessary changes in his attitudes.

Feelings and emotions are important motivating forces in the personality. The more the religious counselor can learn about them and their operation both within himself and within the counselee, the more effective he will be as a counselor.

References

[1] D. O. Hebb, *A Textbook of Psychology* (Philadelphia: W. B. Saunders Co., 1966), p. 235.

[2] Gordon W. Allport, *Pattern and Growth in Personality* (New York: Holt, Rinehart & Winston, Inc., 1961), pp. 198–99.

[3] H. B. English and A. C. English, *A Comprehensive Dictionary of Psychological and Psychoanalytic Terms* (New York: Longmans, Green & Co., 1958).

[4] Magda B. Arnold, *Emotion and Personality* (New York: Columbia University Press, 1960), pp. 74–75.

[5] Ernest R. Hilgard and Richard C. Atkinson, *Introduction to Psychology*, 4th ed. (New York: Harcourt, Brace & World, Inc., 1967), p. 163.

[6] *Ibid.*, p. 163–64.

[7] F. J. Buytendijk, "The Phenomenological Approach to the Problem of Feelings and Emotions," in M. L. Reymert, *Feelings and Emotions* (New York: McGraw-Hill Book Company, 1950), p. 133.

[8] Arnold, *op. cit.*, p. 194.

[9] *Ibid.*, p. 210.

[10] Hebb, *op. cit.*, p. 239.

[11] K. M. Bridges, "Emotional Development in Early Infancy," *Child Development*, III (1932) 324–41.

[12] Clifford T. Morgan and Richard A. King, *Introduction to Psychology* (New York: McGraw-Hill Book Company, 1966), p. 243.

[13] James C. Coleman, *Personality Dynamics and Effective Behavior* (Chicago: Scott, Foresman & Company, 1960), p. 325.

[14] Morgan and King, *op. cit.*, p. 246.

[15] English and English, *op. cit.*, p. 2.

[16] Arnold, *op. cit.*, p. 258.

[17] Hilgard and Atkinson, *op. cit.*, p. 183–84.

[18] *Ibid.*, p. 178.

[19] Arnold, *op. cit.*, p. 272.

[20] Coleman, *op. cit.*, p. 333.

[21] Arnold, *op. cit.*, p. 269.

[22] Harry Overstreet and Bonaro Overstreet, *The Mind Goes Forth* (New York: W. W. Norton & Company, 1956), p. 68.

[23] Coleman, *op. cit.*, p. 334.

[24] R. L. Jenkins, "Guilt Feelings—Their Function and Dysfunction," in M. L. Reymert, *Feeling and Emotion* (New York: McGraw-Hill Book Company, 1950), p. 353.

[25] Coleman, *op. cit.* pp. 336–37.

[26] Dorothy Rethingshafer, *Motivation as Related to Personality* (New York: McGraw-Hill Book Company, 1963), pp. 150–55.

[27] André Godin, S.J., *The Pastor As Counselor* (New York: Holt, Rinehart & Winston, Inc., 1965).

10

Needs of the Counselee

The success of a counselor can be measured by his ability to perceive and meet each counselee's needs. Individuals coming for religious counseling have a definite purpose, although they may not be fully aware of it. One of the primary tasks of a religious counselor is to establish why this individual sought him out for counseling. If he neglects to do this and instead begins by giving advice or applying previously mastered counseling techniques, he will demonstrate to the counselee that he has failed to perceive his true thoughts and feelings. The possibility of establishing a working relationship will be lessened and the session will probably end in an impasse.

The beginning of full communication is mutual acceptance. In religious counseling, the counselee may accept the counselor's position and respect him because of his dedication to God. The counselee will then be able to talk freely about himself and his problem. Or, better still, the counselee may accept the religious counselor because he quickly realizes that the counselor is sincerely concerned about him. He accepts the counselor because the counselor accepts him. In this case the acceptance is built upon mutual trust and regard. In either case, without acceptance on the part of the counselee little communication can take place.

Reasons for Seeking Counseling

People come to the religious counselor for a variety of reasons. Some want information and advice. They may be in doubt about some phase of their belief and may hope that the clergyman as a professional in the field of religion will be able to dispel the doubt. Some are seeking another person to lean on during a period of crisis. Some want to discuss an already formulated decision with a trustworthy, objective observer. Some are looking for someone on whom they can unload their troubles and hostilities. Some are seeking better self-understanding to solve a personal problem. And finally, some come for the explicit purpose of furthering their spiritual development. In a sense each person has a unique reason for seeking counseling. The counselor's success or failure may depend on how quickly he can detect the true reason for the contact—and in view of the complexities of human motivation this is not always an easy task. Theodore Reik has written a book called *Listening With A Third Ear,* in which he describes the various levels of awareness that the competent therapist should have.[1] By the phrase "listening with a third ear," Reik means listening not only with one's ears but with all one's perceptive powers. Perhaps no other phase in religious counseling demands listening with the third ear as much as the beginning one. The effective counselor is like a music lover who is keenly aware of the harmonies and counter melodies as well as the main melody.[2] He hears not only what the counselee says, but how and under what circumstances he says it. He is aware not only of the words that are spoken but also of the feelings and emotions that underlie these words. He notices the intensity and the force with which these words are spoken as well as the counselee's general attitude during the interview. Using all the perceptive skills at his command, the counselor decides upon the probable need which prompted the counselee to seek his help. If the counselee needs some advice about whether he must make restitution after an illegal business deal, the counselor should give the advice rather than withholding it because he thinks a client-centered approach would be more effective. In this case the counselee's main need is to receive advice. If he does not receive it, he will go away feeling frustrated and misunderstood. Perhaps he will seek out another counselor or will give up and try to live with his guilt feelings.

The Beginning Phase

No counselor can absorb and respond to everything that goes on in an interview, especially during the beginning phases when both people are trying to adjust to each other. "Even the most sensitive, experienced, and highly trained practitioner probably responds to a small part of what is actually transpiring." [3] However, the efficient counselor has sufficient skill to make a tentative decision about why the counselee has come. This decision is usually validated later and determines his approach to the interview.

The majority of those who seek religious counseling fall within the range of normality. Among psychologists and psychiatrists, normality is a hotly contested term. We shall use the word *normal*, however, to describe an individual who is able to function adequately in most areas of everyday living.[4] He is relatively successful at work, in his family life, in his social contacts, and in his relationship with God. At present he may need help from someone to face a specific problem, but his overall adjustment is good. The religious counselor can, therefore, assume that he is dealing with a normal person. If he is wrong, he will realize it as the interview progresses and can then begin to think in terms of a referral to a more qualified professional.

In the initial phase, the counselee may feel insecure, fearful, and defensive; he may show his feelings openly or hide them behind an air of poise and self-confidence.[5] If the counselor quickly assumes an active role and suggests a solution before he has established a working relationship, he will probably amplify the counselee's feelings of inadequacy and cause him to flee the interview. For this reason, the first task in counseling is to establish rapport. The counselor listens actively to the counselee, thereby encouraging communication. Active listening means that the counselor's full attention and concern are centered on what the counselee is saying. While the counselor is listening, he tries to separate the important from the unimportant, to decide what is the primary, immediate need of the counselee, and to determine how he himself should participate in the counseling process.

The Counselor's Attitude

Counseling is not something you do *to* a person, but something you engage in *with* a person. "The word *with* suggests that, rather than being a technique, counseling is a relationship." [6] The primary function of the counselor is not to provide service or advice but rather to give of himself.[7] He gives his time, his interest, his attention, his concern, and his understanding. These are intangibles, yet they contribute to the counseling relationship and help the counselee to alter his attitudes and behavior. Even when the counselor, after a period of active listening, is convinced that the counselee is mainly seeking advice, he will still rely on the relationship previously established; unless the counselee accepts the counselor and feels accepted by him, he will probably not accept the advice or act on it.

Shoben describes the qualities that should characterize a therapeutic relationship.[8] These same qualities apply equally to the relationship in religious counseling.

First of all, he says that in the therapeutic relationship the counselor should reflect warm concern. He should be genuinely interested in the counselee as a person and fully committed to helping him. This does not necessarily imply that he should like the counselee, though such liking will contribute to his success. Some counselees, especially if they are unhappy and troubled, are not likeable. It does mean that he should try to understand as sensitively as possible what the counselee is trying to convey and to respect him as a human being. In religious terms this means that the counselor shows true Christian love for the counselee.

Secondly, the counselor is secure enough himself to permit the counselee complete freedom in choosing the subject and content of the discussion. He is not shocked and threatened by what he hears. He can allow the counselee to work through his most personal feelings, repelling as they may be in some instances, and still continue to accept the counselee as a person.

Finally, the counselor is honest and sincere in his dealings with the counselee. He is constantly trying to determine what the counselee is really saying and how he himself is reacting to it. He tries to make the counselee realize that he does understand what has been expressed. At times, being honest and sincere may mean revealing to the counselee his true feelings, such as self-pity, resentment, guilt, or remorse. Much of the counselor's skill "lies in his ability to combine honesty and directness with a sensitive understanding of the counselee's needs and feelings." [9] The counselor points out limitations but he does not condemn them. The effect on the counselee of the counselor's honesty and sensitivity is a lowering of defenses and a willingness to be open and trusting.[10] In addition to honesty, timing is also important. At one time the counselee may be able to accept a directness that he could not accept at another time.

Language

To demonstrate his understanding and acceptance, the counselor makes use of language that is meaningful to the counselee. Cultural background, socioeconomic level, and education determine language usage. The professional theologian, for example, usually has a larger and more diversified vocabulary than most people. He may use professional terms that are almost unheard of in other groups. Sometimes words may have one meaning in one group and quite a different meaning in another. The counselor must try to understand the language of the counselee from a different background. Most religious counselors are college graduates and have much in common with the professional class; this is an advantage when dealing with people in the same class but can be a disadvantage when counseling people from lower socioeconomic levels. The religious counselor who wishes to work with socioeconomic groups other than his own should gain experience by finding situations which will throw him in with these other groups, so that he can learn their language and outlook.

Once the counselor has listened carefully enough to have an adequate understanding of the counselee's inner world and his reason for seeking help, the next step is to give him an indication that he has been understood. This can often be accomplished by reformulating what the counselee has just said. If the counselor can express the thoughts and feelings of the counselee in clearer and more expressive language, he will help to clarify the counselee's confused thinking. With experience and practice, the counselor learns to reformulate thoughts, feelings, and views succinctly and in the counselee's own language. Through this skill he gives the counselee a more objective view of what is going on within his experiential world. Sometimes it may be unnecessary to reformulate all of what the counselee has said during the initial explanatory stage—concentrating on one aspect may be sufficient. When the counselor uses this procedure to give evidence of an intelligent, sensitive grasp of the important elements under discussion, the counselee knows that his words have been understood. The reformulation thus has a two-fold purpose: (1) It indicates to the counselee that what he has said is understood and respected as something of value; and (2) it helps clarify for the counselee the various aspects of the topic under discussion.

To exemplify the process of reformulation, let us return for a moment to Jane, the eighteen-year-old girl wrestling with the decision about whether she has a true "call" from God to become a nun (see Chapter 7). At the beginning of the session in which Jane brought up the question of a vocation, she said that as a child she felt what she considered a genuine call from God. At that time she was sure that God wanted her to become a nun and her assent made her very happy. She then went on to say: "I have never felt that way since. Lately when I think about entering the convent, I feel as if I have to go or I will let God down. He has given me the grace and I cannot be unfaithful to it." Then she added: "What bothers me is that maybe I feel the same way about my vocation as I do about my studies. I just have to do well in school or I couldn't live with myself. I would be letting my mother and even myself down." The mention of her mother led her to explain that her mother resented even the mention of her intention to enter the convent. "My mother says that I should have more consideration for her and my sisters after all that she has done for me. She says I can think about entering the convent after I finish college. There's plenty of time, she says." The discussion then turned to Peter, the boy she had been dating for almost a year, and the difficulty of saying goodbye to him and meaning it. She finished with the statement: "Some days I am all ready to go ahead with my decision to enter, but the next day I change my mind and say it costs too much; it's not for me. But then I begin to feel guilty because I am not doing what God wants me to do."

By this time Sister Mary was beginning to understand how Jane felt about her situation, and she made the following recapitulation: "You seem to be caught in a bind and you are not sure which way you should go. You are not sure whether it is a lack of courage and fidelity to God that makes you run away from the thought of a vocation, or whether you are afraid to face your mother and go through the pain of giving up Peter. At the same time you wonder whether your vocation is founded on a real calling from God or whether you are being driven to enter the convent by the same kind of feeling that makes you do well in school."

The Point of Decision

The counselor has now reached the point of decision. He must decide what are the most probable reasons for the counselee's coming to his office or rectory parlor. He concentrates mainly on the immediate needs. The religious counselor who has had some training in psychology may detect personality limitations in the counselee requiring intensive therapy, but as a religious counselor he is usually not in a position to offer this kind of help. His time is limited. He has obligations to all the members of his congregation; he cannot afford to concentrate on a few and neglect the others. In addition to counseling he is engaged in many other activities, including administrative duties which occupy a large part of his working day. As a religious counselor his primary task is to meet the counselee's immediate needs and to make him more aware of the spiritual dimension in his problem. It may well happen that when his immediate needs are met, the counselee becomes less neurotic, but the counselor does not set out to accomplish this. We shall now consider the counselee's immediate needs in more detail.

Need for Information

The counselee may have come to the counselor simply to seek information, perhaps about the church's position on a current issue like civil rights. Perhaps the individual has been asked by a fellow worker to participate in a demonstration, and he does not know whether he should; but he feels a certain obligation as a Christian to become involved in the struggle for racial equality. He comes to the religious counselor hoping to find an answer to specific questions involving justice and Christian charity. He is honest in presenting his doubts; he expects similar honesty from the representative of the Church. Effectiveness in this kind of situation demands that the counselor listen on both an intellectual and emotional level without giving any answers until he sees clearly what the counselee wants. He then gives as straightforward and specific an answer as he can. Sometimes the counselee will raise questions and issues for which there are no pat answers. In these instances the counselee expects at least an honest admission that the Church provides no definite answer and an expression of the counselor's personal views.

Some counselees who are ostensibly seeking information actually have other reasons for coming to the counselor. If the counselor listens only on an intellectual level, gives an answer, and terminates the meeting, he has missed an important part of the counselee's communication. It is not uncommon for a person to ask a number of questions on moral issues simply as a means of getting to the real problem. For example, a college student comes to the counselor wondering if he has gone too far in showing affection for his girl-friend. On the surface it would appear that he wants to know what is permitted and what is forbidden, but further listening reveals that he is experiencing some very deep feelings of guilt and needs to express them. The real purpose for his seeking counseling is to unburden himself so that he can live more comfortably with God and himself. If the counselor fails to see this need, the counselee may continue to have guilt feelings, eventually leading to depression. For this reason it is important for the counselor to hear the counselee out before he decides on a course of action. He should not jump in before he clearly understands what the situation requires.

Need for Support

At some time in his life nearly everyone needs to lean temporarily on another person. In these periods of crisis many people turn to a priest, a minister, or perhaps a nun who was a former teacher and confidante. In most cases, once the crisis has passed the individual is able to stand on his own without support. He regains his equilibrium and continues his life grateful for the counselor's act of charity. Had he been unable to find support during his time of need, he might well have been completely overwhelmed and might have taken much longer to recover his balance.[11]

The supportive function is one of the more important functions of the religious counselor. The individual who is overcome by grief at the loss of a wife or a child, who has just come to a new city and feels lost, or who is guilt-ridden as a result of a misdeed, often needs someone on whom he can lean until he regains his inner strength. The average person has neither the inclination nor the money to go to a psychiatrist or a clinical psychologist during every period of crisis. And even if he did, he probably could not find a psychiatrist with enough time to meet all his immediate needs. Moreover, many people do not want to reveal their inner feelings and weaknesses to a professional therapist during a period of trial. They look to the clergyman for help. If the religious counselor understands and meets the immediate need of the counselee, he performs through a few simple procedures an invaluable service. The purpose of supportive counseling is to bring the individual back to normal emotional equilibrium as soon as possible with a minimum of damage to his personality.[12]

Ways of Supporting the Counselee

There are many ways in which the religious counselor can be supportive. One is simply by being present in a special time of need. His presence is equivalent to saying "You are not alone; I am here as a source of help whenever you might need me." [13] A word of reassurance or understanding is often sufficient to give the counselee strength to bear a seemingly intolerable burden.

When death occurs in a family, the religious counselor is frequently called upon to be supportive. His concern becomes a source of strength to the bereaved persons. Supportive counseling can also take more explicit forms. The counselor may express open approval of the counselee's actions; he may compliment him on a wise decision; or he may identify with the counselee's feelings about a particular situation, saying, "If I were in your position, I would have been angry too" or "You are right to be angry." He may also give support at a time of indecision. Some people are afflicted with indecisiveness and find it extremely difficult to make almost any important decision, but once they have acted they usually can follow through with relative ease. Psychologists call this "vestibule" anxiety

—anxiety expressed on the threshold of any new situation. Once the situation has been confronted, the anxiety disappears. Sometimes the function of the religious counselor is to help the individual over the threshold by reassurance or persuasion. The goal of such supportive counseling is not to make the counselee dependent but to make him stand on his own as quickly as possible. Since this type of counseling usually requires an authoritarian relationship, however, the counselor should avoid the danger of encouraging the counselee to overevaluate the counselor's ability to make a decision and to play down his own.[14]

The effects of supportive counseling are threefold. First of all it helps to reduce the level of anxiety.[15] When an individual is highly anxious, his efficiency is reduced. If the anxiety can be lessened, he will be better able to make a decision and to act. Moreover, as we stated in a previous chapter, anxiety tends to restrict one's view of the world and of himself. Under such circumstances the individual will lack the capacity to take a constructive step forward. A second effect of supportive counseling is to arouse self-assurance. Some individuals need to be persuaded that they can succeed. Once they have experienced success, they no longer need the support. A final effect of this type of counseling is to keep the counselee from following a destructive course of action. When a person is greatly threatened, he is more likely to follow impulse than reason. To thwart the impulsive act, the counselor is sometimes forced to use pressure and coercion.

Dangers of Supportive Counseling

In making use of supportive measures, the counselor should always keep in mind their limitations.[16] Perhaps the greatest danger is that the counselee may become dependent on the counselor. Some individuals are so psychologically weak that they have a constant need to lean on other people. They tend to seek out the priest or minister, attach themselves to him, and expect him to take over their lives. Consequently, the religious counselor should guard against becoming trapped in such a relationship, which can consume much time for little purpose. Often this kind of relationship is accompanied by underlying hostility and guilt. Once the counselee becomes aware of how dependent he actually is on the counselor, he often begins to feel even more inadequate and subsequently experiences a deep resentment. It is imperative that the counselor take steps to disengage himself from a dependency relationship that is growing too strong.

Another danger is that the evident shallowness of some supportive measures can destroy all confidence in the counselor. For example, a stereotyped comment like "Everything will turn out fine, so don't worry," has already been offered by other people when things did not turn out fine. As far as the counselee is concerned, these are just words intended to make him feel better, but with little or no validity. They lessen his respect for the counselor. Certain situations call for supportive counseling to help a person over a particularly rough period, but the counselor should be constantly on guard against doing more harm than good with this technique.

Counseling as
an Opportunity to Talk

Frequently the visitor to the religious counselor's office or rectory just wants to talk with someone. He is vaguely aware of something bothering him, but he is not so upset that he could not handle it on his own if he had to. His immediate need is to get something "off his chest." He seeks out the religious counselor because he feels that the religious counselor can be trusted and will show some understanding. Merely talking out a problem often clears the air and makes it seem less disturbing. Talking can be therapeutic.[17] After a discussion, the counselee often feels that he has a better understanding of all the factors involved and that he can exercise self-control and mastery. The counselor may think that his role as an understanding listener is relatively inconsequential or even a waste of time, whereas actually it may be the most productive hour he spends all day. Even people who are usually capable of handling ordinary problems on their own occasionally become emotionally "fed-up." After unburdening themselves they can continue to lead relatively successful lives. The counselor need only listen actively and indicate some understanding.[18] By giving of himself he may play a significant role in making the counselee a happier person.

Sometimes the counselee spends his time talking about some

disturbing event, such as a family quarrel or an angry exchange of words with the boss. Throwing himself into the description causes him to reexperience this event and to experience for the first time feelings and emotions that were formerly repressed. He can recreate the experience in a more objective way because of the support and acceptance of the counselor.[19] He is no longer nearly as threatened and can see more satisfying and constructive ways of acting. Many of his anxieties are released. Afterwards he can go back to his family or job with an air of confidence, convinced that with a little adjustment he can master a previously disturbing situation.

Counseling as
Confirmation of Decisions

Sometimes an individual comes to the religious counselor to check out the logic of his own reasoning. He looks upon the counselor as an intelligent, prudent person and respects his judgment. Although he may have little doubt about the wisdom of his own decision, he wants to validate it further by exposing it to the views of another person. The counselor should perceive that this is the primary purpose for the contact and then furnish clear, precise statements of his opinions. Refusing to give the counselee what he seeks—because of a fear of creating a dependency relationship or because of a conviction that the nondirective approach would be more effective—merely produces frustration and a loss of regard for the counselor. Actually if the counselor perceives the counselee's purpose accurately, there is little danger of lasting dependency ties. The counselee realizes that he has the ability to act from reason; he simply thinks it wiser to check this reasoning against that of an objective observer. No one sees things with complete accuracy; another person's view can draw attention to one's inaccuracies.

Client-Centered Approach

Carl Rogers, a prominent figure in contemporary psychology, was among the first to investigate what takes place when two people talk over a personal matter, one showing anxiety over his situation and the other experiencing regard, concern, and empathy for him.[20] From his findings has come a system known as client-centered counseling, which has much to offer the religious counselor helping normal people with everyday problems. "Client-centered therapy is built on two essential hypotheses; (1) the individual has within himself the capacity, at least latent, to understand the factors in his life which cause him unhappiness and pain and to reorganize himself in such a way as to overcome these factors; (2) these powers will become effective if the therapist can establish with the client a relationship sufficiently warm, accepting, and understanding." [21] If one accepts these two assumptions (which are solidly supported by research findings) the client-centered approach is logical and sensible. In this approach, the counselor concerns himself with trying to understand the counselee's world as the counselee does. He tries "to perceive with him his confusions, fears, and ambitions."

He is concerned not with judging or making suggestions but with trying to understand the counselee. He accepts the counselee's views as those of a person of worth and dignity. Although he may not agree with these views, he respects the individual's right to express himself and does not reject him. In this atmosphere of psychological security, the counselee can afford to examine every ramification of his problem without fear of being threatened or hurt. Most important, he dares to look within himself and see that part of himself, disgusting as it may be, which is the main cause of the problem. He no longer needs to look at a distorted or completely false image of himself or to change the world to fit his distorted needs.[22] He can face his actual view of and feelings about the situation. He can then bring the whole matter into the open, see it in its true perspective, acknowledge his own part in it, and work toward a resolution. He has the objective facts, the raw material for making a valid decision. He can do this without a need for the counselor to suggest possible alternatives of action or to judge what he thinks would be the best way to act. Such an approach demands an implicit faith in the counselee's ability to arrive at a decision by himself in a favorable psychological atmosphere.

The client-centered approach used by clinical psychologists differs in depth and intensity from that used by the religious counselor. A clinical psychologist following the Rogerian method is trying to affect personality change through better self-acceptance; the religious counselor is trying to help the counselee handle everyday problems and discover the promptings of the Spirit. The clergyman who becomes proficient in the client-centered approach can greatly enhance his effectiveness, however. He quickly learns from experience that with many counselees this is the most successful counseling procedure. At the same time he should keep in mind that a rigid adherence to any one approach can destroy his effectiveness and that his primary concern should be to determine and meet the counselee's immediate needs.

Let us consider a brief sequence in a counseling session to demonstrate how the client-centered counselor reacts.

Jane: I hate to talk about this matter of a vocation. I've avoided it for months. Every time I think of it, I get more confused and down.

Sister Mary: It is really painful and upsetting to have to talk about this.

Jane: It sure is. I don't know whether I should enter in September or not. Sometimes I think I would make a great nun and at other times I say to myself that I do not have what it takes. Anyway it costs too much and besides I wonder whether this is what I really want.

Sister Mary: You find yourself in a real bind. Should I enter or should I forget the whole thing?

Jane: Every time I try to convince myself that it is not for me, I begin to feel guilty, as if I am doing something that I shouldn't. Then I turn around and convince myself that God has given me this grace and I can't turn Him down. I start thinking about how short life really is. In a few years I will be dead and then the only thing that will count is whether I saved my soul.

Sister Mary: Sometimes you do everything you can to convince yourself that you do have a vocation but then you suspect you might be doing this so you won't feel guilty.

Jane: I wish I could make up my mind and get back to being my old happy self again. I hate this going back and forth and never coming to any definite decision. It really gets me down. If I could just have someone tell me: you have a vocation or you don't have a vocation, I think that I would get my peace of mind back again.

Sister Mary: You just wish it were possible for me or someone else to give you a foolproof answer about what you should do.

In this sequence Jane talks about her troubling indecisiveness and Sister Mary indicates that she is trying to grasp the way Jane feels. Sister Mary is content with trying to understand what Jane is experiencing at the moment. She offers no suggestions or advice.

Need-Centered Approach

Some counselees are so caught up in indecision that left to themselves they flounder about aimlessly. The client-centered approach often drags on and on with little apparent progress. Sometimes it is necessary to give a clear statement of the alternatives with the pros and cons for each, perhaps followed by a little push toward a decision. At other times, the confusion and indecision have reached such a state that the individual is at an impasse but because of circumstances must make a decision. This case requires some kind of intervention by the counselor. For example, a young woman who is to be married the following morning comes to the rectory hopelessly confused and tearful. She does not know whether she should go ahead with the ceremony. Every time she settles on one alternative, she begins to waver and an hour or so later reverts to a state of indecision. Now she is coming down to the wire and must make an irrevocable decision, but she feels incapable of making it. In such a situation the counselor may have to become very direct, to the point of insisting on a course of action. Again, the counselee's need determines the approach.

As we have seen, each counselee has his own frame of reference. He looks at the world in a unique way, and this outlook has become set with repetition and the passing of time. Not all of one's frame of reference is consistent with objective reality. We all develop some faulty views and attitudes. Since these have become a part of the personality structure, we are loath to give them up. The way a convinced Christian looks upon his religion is an integral part of himself and his general view of life. He will probably not abandon this view without a struggle. Similarly, a man who has lost his trust of people and who sees everyone as fundamentally evil—as liars, cheats, and thieves—has made this view of the human race an integral part of his frame of reference and will not easily part with it.

The religious counselor sometimes meets a person with a faulty or distorted frame of reference who is convinced that his view is the correct one. Talking about it fails to effect any change in the counselee, or perhaps makes him even more determined. In this case, the religious counselor may do better if he abandons the client-centered approach and becomes more directive. The counselee needs to have someone whom he respects point out the flaws in his attitudes. He sometimes needs the opportunity to compare his frame of reference with someone else's. Only through an awareness of how he differs from other people will he begin to question the validity of his own stand.

An example might be an individual who is a perfectionist and who does either a superb job or nothing. Although he thinks this is a laudatory way to act, he thinks he is constantly failing; he seldom lives up to his self-imposed standards and often neglects his obligations and responsibilities. He comes to his pastor complaining that he is a failure in his family life—a poor husband and a worse father. The more he talks, the more convinced he appears to be of his own failings; but at the same time the evidence he offers shows that he is a better-than-average family man. Inasmuch as the counselee is so inflexible, the pastor may have to become more directive than he would like to, focusing on the faulty frame of reference and suggesting that it does not fit objective facts.

The Religious Dimension

Religious counseling has as its ultimate goal the counselee's spiritual improvement. This is true even in handling every day problems which appear to be far from spiritual. As we have seen, every situation has a religious dimension. Often the counselee will see this dimension on his own if the religious counselor is a warm, accepting, and understanding person. At times, however, he may become so thoroughly involved in the material aspects that he overlooks the spiritual ones. The religious counselor must then point out the spiritual significance of the situation. As we have previously stated, religious counseling is basically value counseling, since it is intended to inculcate or strengthen religious and moral values. The counselee expects that the spiritual dimensions of the matter under discussion will be recognized in some explicit fashion.

It is often for this reason that he seeks out the religious counselor in preference to the psychologist or psychiatrist.

The religious dimension might also be described as a testing of the Spirit. God moves each of us in His own way. It is up to us to discover how God is prompting us and what He asks of us. One function of religious counseling is to prepare the counselee to listen to the divine promptings. This can sometimes be achieved by helping the counselee come to better self-understanding, which includes an understanding of God as a direct or indirect influence on his thoughts and actions. Many counselees can achieve this goal through a client-centered approach. Others, however, need the guidance of an experienced spiritual director who has the capacity to point out evidence of the Spirit working in the counselee's everyday life.

We have seen that the counselor first determines what the counselee needs and what prompted him to seek counseling and then finds appropriate means to meet these needs. In the final chapter, we shall consider several ways to recognize and help the abnormal person.

References

[1] Theodore Reik, *Listening with the Third Ear* (New York: Grove Press, 1948).

[2] J. G. Watkins, "Psychotherapeutic Methods," in *Handbook of Clinical Psychology*, ed. B. J. Wolman (New York: McGraw-Hill Book Company, 1965).

[3] *Ibid.*, p. 1153.

[4] Gordon W. Allport, *Patterns and Growth in Personality* (New York: Holt, Rinehart & Winston, Inc., 1961), pp. 150–51.

[5] Charles A. Curran, "Structuring the Counseling Relationship: A Case Report," *Journal of Abnormal and Social Psychology*, XXXIX (1944), 189–216.

[6] C. H. Patterson, "Counseling as a Relationship," *Journal of Rehabilitation* (Nov.–Dec., 1959), pp. 13–15.

[7] *Ibid.*, p. 14.

[8] E. J. Shoben, "A Theoretical Approach to Psychotherapy as a Personality Modification," *Harvard Educational Review*, XXIII (1953), 128–42.

[9] *Ibid.*, p. 137.

[10] W. E. Cottle, "Some Common Elements in Counseling," *Personnel and Guidance Journal*, XXXII (1953), 4–8.

[11] F. C. Thorne, *Principles of Personality Counseling* (Brandon, Vermont: *Journal of Clinical Psychology*, 1950), p. 201.

[12] Lewis R. Wolberg, *The Technique of Psychotherapy*, Part II (New York: Grune & Stratton, Inc., 1967).

[13] Leopold Bellak, *Emergency Psychotherapy and Brief Psychotherapy* (New York: Grune & Stratton, Inc., 1965), pp. 62–63.

[14] Wolberg, *op. cit.*, p. 17.

[15] Lawrence M. Brammer and Everett L. Shostrom, *Therapeutic Psychology* (Englewood Cliffs, N.J.: Prentice-Hall, Inc., 1960), p. 167.

[16] *Ibid.*, p. 169.

[17] Watkins, *op. cit.*, p. 1160.

[18] *Ibid.*, p. 1159.

[19] *Ibid.*, p. 1160.

[20] Carl R. Rogers, *Client-Centered Therapy* (Boston: Houghton Mifflin Company, 1951).

[21] Carl R. Rogers, "Client-Centered Psychotherapy," *Scientific American* (November, 1952).

[22] Carl R. Rogers, "Therapy, Personality and Interpersonal Relationships," in *Psychology, A Study of Science* (Vol. 3), ed. Sigmund Koch (New York: McGraw-Hill Book Company, 1959).

11

The Abnormal Person

The people who visit the parish rectory or the religious counselor's office come from all walks of life, present a wide variety of problems, and possess many levels of mental health or illness. One of the major tasks of the religious counselor is to sort out those who are capable of responding to his concern from those who need more intensive and specialized care. Usually the clergyman is not trained in psychiatry or clinical psychology; even if he were, he would not have the time to provide extensive treatment. Nevertheless, the mentally and emotionally ill come to him seeking relief from their neurotic or psychotic symptoms, and he should know how he can be of greatest service to them.

Recognizing the Mentally Ill

Who are the mentally and emotionally ill? As we have previously indicated, the answer to this question is still debated. To have a working definition, we shall describe the mentally ill as people who are unable to function adequately as human beings. They are unable "to work out the balanced give and take required for sound friendship, for smooth relations at work, and domestic felicity." [1] They fail again and again to adjust to everyday situations. Often they have few or no friends; their marital lives are in a state of crisis; and their employment history is erratic. Often their symptoms and patterns of behavior single them out as different. They are closed in upon themselves and are unable to reach out to other people. They are often driven by seemingly uncontrollable emotions and impulses, and their condition is chronic rather than periodic.

Traditionally mental illness has been classified into three types: (1) Psychosis, (2) Psychoneurosis, and (3) Personality or character disorders.[2] Psychosis, which is considered the most severe type, is characterized by drastic changes in feeling, thought, and behavior. The psychotic usually withdraws from reality to live in a world of his own creation. He often experiences persistent delusions or hallucinations. In contrast, psychoneurosis is an emotional disorder resulting from an inability to cope with anxiety. The psychoneurotic is usually a tense, unhappy, and chronically fatigued person. To offset the mental sufferings caused by anxiety, he may defend himself through irrational fears, obsessions, compulsions, and imagined illnesses. Personality disorder is characterized by warped emotional development. The individual who suffers from this disorder often has insufficient feelings of guilt, seldom learns from experience, and forms few meaningful relationships. He is usually egocentric. This classification includes the drug addict, the chronic alcoholic, and the delinquent.

The function of the religious counselor is not to offer treatment but to recognize that the individual is mentally ill and to make the proper referral. The counselor can make such a referral only if he knows how to recognize the signs of mental illness. We shall therefore consider some typical signs of mental illness and some specific mental illnesses that the religious counselor may meet in his daily contact with counselees.

Signs of Psychosis

The signs of psychotic behavior are well described in a pamphlet issued by the National Association of Mental Health:

1. The individual manifests radical changes in his way of thinking and acting. He may have been a person who had always been a serious, respected member of the community but who suddenly becomes quite quarrelsome, stays out late at night, or gambles

with a group with whom he never before had any association. Or he may become persistently antagonistic, get into frequent fights, or, on the other hand, become unusually happy for no apparent reason. He may even become so preoccupied with apparently unimportant matters that he is too busy to eat or sleep.

In most instances, he is unaware of the sudden change in his behavior and may become antagonistic when this is called to his attention. However, this markedly changed behavior can usually be verified by those close to him. They usually have also noticed this difference and generally are aware when it appears to be continuing.

2. He has strange periods of confusion or loss of memory. All of us go through fleeting moments of being forgetful about the day or week or we are unable to recall the name of a friend. The psychotic person, however, may repeatedly forget who he is, that he is married, or what day or month of the year it is. He may even have difficulty in telling you where he is or where he was a few days ago.

It is not unusual for a mentally ill person to have disturbances of memory. He is so worried and involved with his own problems that he does not notice calendars, whistles blowing in the morning and evening, church bells ringing, or even hunger pains in his stomach.

3. He thinks people are plotting against him or he has grandiose ideas about himself. The mentally ill person may believe that the people with whom he works are plotting to get him fired, or he may become very aggressive toward these fellow employees because of such unfounded thoughts. He may also think that others whom he doesn't even know are plotting against him. Or he may believe that all activities in the factory would cease if he missed one day's work, even though his job is quite simple and his absence would not at all affect the smooth operation within the factory. Another way of showing this disturbance may be to consider himself an important religious or political leader. Or he may think that he is a great scientist inventing the drug to cure major ills in the world. Once again, discussion with this person's family can reveal that his claims are quite exaggerated and untrue.

4. He talks to himself and hears voices. Many people on occasion talk quietly to themselves when they are alone. However, the psychotic person may talk vigorously to himself even though there are many people around him. He may tell you with the utmost sincerity that he is responding to a voice that is talking solely to him. Some persons having these experiences may suddenly stray off into the distance, or they may interrupt a conversation or an activity to respond to the voice that they hear. Bringing to the ill person's attention that there are no such imaginary voices will do no good.

He may persist in hearing these voices and may vehemently resist the suggestion that it is just his imagination.

5. He thinks people are watching him or talking about him. In the early stages of some mental illness, the person may be quite sensitive, and feel that his movements are being watched, and that the people in the community discuss him. Sometimes he may walk in the street, pass a group of people and be certain that they are talking about him. Or on the bus, he is convinced that other riders are staring at him. Although there is no truth to these ideas, he genuinely feels that he is justified in his suspicions. As the illness develops, he becomes increasingly convinced that his ideas are true, and that more and more people are involved.

6. He complains of bodily changes that are not possible. He may think that his heart is actually not beating, or that he is suffering from a rare fatal disease. He may believe that his face is disfigured or that he is immuned to pain and other sensations. These complaints are so real to him that he may go to the doctor repeatedly. However, continued reassurance without other skilled help is rarely of any avail. A mentally ill person suffers from these symptoms nearly as much as if they were actually caused by some disease.

7. He suffers from the needs to perform several repetitive acts many times over and is plagued by many foreboding thoughts. He may have a morbid fear of germs, and spend an inordinate amount of time in such acts as washing every time he touches a book, a door-knob, a dollar bill, or any object handled by other people. Or he may be possessed with a terrible thought that he will do harm to a member of his family. There are innumerable repetitive acts or foreboding thoughts that may preoccupy a mentally ill person. He becomes terribly upset if he is prevented from carrying out these repetitive acts and finds it nearly impossible to eliminate the morbid thoughts from his mind regardless of what he is told.

8. He shows marked depressed behavior. Almost everyone at some time feels "blue" or discouraged; these are normal reactions, following some loss. The clergyman meets many normal periods of discouragement in his ministry to the bereaved. However, some depressed persons are severely ill. They suffer from a far greater, more profound disruption of personality.

Most often under the impact of self-directed hostility, an individual may present a variety of complaints representing a collapse of the inner core of self-esteem. He may feel utterly worthless and alone. He may sit for hours not speaking or moving, with his head hung down in an air of complete dejection. When he speaks or moves he may do so with marked retardation—heavy, plodding steps, pained countenance. If he is able to talk, he may indicate his feeling that he is very low, that he has committed an unpardonable sin. Occasionally one encounters persons in great agitation and excitement giving voice to the same complaints of overwhelming worthlessness. These persons are severely ill. Members of the family and acquaintances who have been close to such severely depressed people may be able to recount a number of recent near accidents or injuries. Sometimes the person is able to tell of his worthlessness in terms of his inability to control his angry or destructive thoughts towards those whom he loves. He may actually give up hope and think of suicide. The fact that such a person is able to talk of suicide is definitely no assurance that he will not make an attempt to do so.

The clergyman's attempts to cheer this severely ill person, to get him to look more positively at the world, are almost certain to fail. A rest, a vacation from responsibility, even little kindnesses are more likely to aggravate than help. These are critical emergencies and the person suffering requires the protection from himself and the subsequent treatment that can usually be secured only from skilled medical care. When a clergyman encounters a person whose severe depression has begun to "lift" without treatment, he should recall that this period of early recovery is one of the times of greatest danger from suicide.

9. He behaves in a way that is dangerous to others. The number of such incidents is slight, but a mentally ill person may decide to hurt another person whom he feels is persecuting him. An individual suffering from such a disorder may tell a convincing story of how he is being abused by another, even though there is repeated reassurance that this person is in no way involved and could not possibly do such a thing. Still, the disturbed person is not convinced.

Most clergymen who read the above list are undoubtedly aware of persons in the community who may display one or more of these symptoms. It is well to remember that many of these people may have been living with some of these symptoms over a long period of time and do not need special attention. No service will be done by disturbing the marginal adjustment of such persons, as long as their eccentric but continuing adjustment does not become upset. It is only when the symptoms become exaggerated or when there is a sudden onset of other symptoms that there is any occasion for pastoral concern, and then one should first get expert advice.

When the clergyman is confronted with a person who is full of despair and has lost contact with reality, it is well, when the opportunity presents itself, to state simply the way in which he sees the situation, and indicate that he realizes this is not the way that the disturbed person sees it. Thus, an individual who declares bitterly his conviction that "the communists are digging a subway under the church" is met by the clergyman's matter-of-fact, "I do not feel that we are threatened by anything mysterious, but I can understand that you feel you are under some pressure."

Almost never is there any occasion for the clergyman to agree with or dispute heatedly the distortions of reality that a disturbed person may present. When the person has "lost contact with reality," skillful psychiatric help is needed to help him resume contact with those around, and referral to a professional treatment source should be made.[3]

Signs of Psychoneurosis

Some indications of the neurotic personality can be summarized as follows:

1. The individual shows signs of tension.[4] He is on edge much of the time and feels that he is all tied up. He may experience twitching and jumping muscles or his hands may shake. He may complain of frequent headaches.

2. He is unhappy and depressed. Most of us experience periods when things are not going right and we become depressed, but these periods are infrequent and the depression lasts for a relatively short period of time. The neurotic person is chronically unhappy and miserable. His depressions are frequent and can last for several days or even weeks. Frequently he does not know why he feels so miserable, but he knows that to him life does not seem worth living.

3. He feels tired much of the time, yet he suffers from insomnia. For no apparent reason he feels exhausted. In the mornings he wakes up feeling tired and drags himself through the day, but at night he finds it difficult to sleep. Sometimes he awakens during the early hours of the morning and cannot get back to sleep.

4. He is hounded by worries and fears. Feelings of inadequacy and inferiority place him under great pressure in most of his undertakings. He fears and worries about failure. Many of his worries center around health. He is afraid that he is going insane or that he has heart trouble.

5. He finds it difficult to get along with other people. The idiosyncrasies of other people get on his nerves, and his get on

theirs. He has few friends and may lose the few that he has. He prefers to be alone, but he dreads loneliness.

6. He may experience obsessions and compulsions. He may be scrupulously fearful of committing a sin against charity or justice or may see sin in everything he does. He may be driven to repeat certain actions over and over again, like washing his hands many times a day to free himself from germs.

The neurotic may mention some of these symptoms during the interview; some may become evident from his actions; or a relative may indicate concern about his behavior. The religious counselor should try to understand the neurotic's frame of reference and to show empathy. The counselor is not in a position to alter the neurotic's state of mind or to relieve his symptoms, because they spring from deep-seated psychological causes. An appeal for greater faith or perseverance in prayer has little or no effect, since the neurotic is in need of psychotherapy. The religious counselor should concentrate on directing the neurotic to the psychiatrist's office.

Personality Disorder

The individual with a personality disorder who seeks out the clergyman is often in trouble with the law or with his relatives. Often it is not the person himself who comes to the counselor, but a distraught mother or wife asking for help in coping with the erratic, antisocial behavior of a son or husband. More often than not, the personality disorder can also be described as a psychopathic personality. Some of the signs of the psychopathic personality are included in the following list:

1. He is egocentric.[5] He does not look to the good of others but is wholly concerned with his own pleasure. He lives only for himself and his wife and children really make no difference to him. He can "fall in love" with another woman and abandon his family with seemingly no qualms of conscience. He can become highly indignant when another person suggests that he has obligations to support his family. Intellectually he may condemn his actions, but in fact he follows his impulses like a child. The only meaningful control in his life is the threat of punishment.

2. His actions are unbalanced. He follows impulse rather than reason. He may get the urge to invest all his family funds in

a wild scheme and does so without giving the matter a thought. He is always hoping for the big financial kill. He may cash bad checks to pull himself out of a debt or to support himself and his family.

3. He is emotionally unstable. He is likely to blow up at any little thing or to be overwhelmed with joy over some insignificant event. He swings easily from excessive confidence to complete discouragement.

4. He often has a very appealing personality when one first meets him. He has the ability to sell himself to other people, but the better they know him, the more disturbed they become about him.

5. He is able to lie, cheat and steal, and think nothing of it. His general attitude is "the world owes me a living, so whatever I take from someone else is really mine." He does not seem to learn from experience. He can be apprehended and sentenced to a jail term only to return to the same type of activity as soon as he is released. He seems to have little anxiety or guilt. He can engage in flagrant misconduct, such as weeks of constant drinking or sexual promiscuity, and see no reason why he should not continue this activity.

6. He is unreliable and irresponsible.[6] He has little insight and cannot foresee the consequences of his actions. He fails to understand on an emotional level that he is doing wrong. As a result, he is frequently incensed when he is punished for his behavior because he sees no reason for the punishment.

The psychopathic person is an extremely difficult individual to cope with because he is so adept at manipulating people. Unless the religious counselor has some understanding of this type of personality, he may be taken in and manipulated in such a way that he furthers the irresponsible and impulsive behavior. After the counselor has realized what type of person he is dealing with, he should act with firmness and definiteness. He should be alert to the ways he is being manipulated. Some psychopathic persons are superficially pious and frequent church services, but often they do this to gain their own ends. As with the psychotic and neurotic, the major task of the religious counselor is to make a good psychiatric referral. An attempt to use religious means to change the behavior of the psychopath will probably end in frustration.

Let us now consider three cases exemplifying these three types of mental or emotional illness and the methods the religious counselor should use in handling them.

A *Psychotic Reaction*

Mrs. M., a forty-year-old woman who has been married seventeen years and has four children ranging in age from three to fifteen, comes to the rectory for advice. She is very distraught and upset. During the past five years, her husband has been growing more and more suspicious of her. He now accuses her of being unfaithful to her marriage vows and running around with other men and says that he can prove it. He is consistently nagging at her and telling her that everything she does is wrong. She finds it impossible to please him in any way. She cannot see anything in her behavior that would provoke this type of abuse. She maintains that she has always been faithful to him. Although he never physically attacks her, the constant persecution is becoming intolerable; she endures it only for the sake of her children.

A week later the husband comes to the rectory, saying that he wants to talk about a personal matter. During the first ten minutes what he says is vague and incomprehensible. His thoughts are disjointed and the counselor is at a loss to know why he has come. He then begins to talk about a special revelation he has received from God through a new electronic device which he has invented and which is able to penetrate minds. By using this device, he has penetrated the mind of God and has discovered something very important for the welfare of the whole Church. He is convinced that he must tell the Bishop what he has discovered in order to avert a great catastrophe in the Church. He wants the counselor to set up an appointment with the Bishop. When pressed to explain the impending catastrophe, he simply states that he cannot tell the counselor any more about the matter, since it pertains only to himself, God, and the Bishop. At no time during the interview does he mention his marital difficulties; probably he is not even aware of his wife's previous visit to the rectory.

This case illustrates a psychotic reaction. The husband is mentally ill and his behavior is symptomatic of his illness. He is beyond the reach of counseling and needs intensive psychiatric care. To be of help, the religious counselor must first realize that this individual is psychotic (or to use nontechnical language, insane). Since his thinking is paranoid, there is a great need for the counselor to be honest and avoid deviousness. Nothing can be gained by agreeing with his distorted views. If the counselor is convinced that the counselee is deluded, he should say so. He might put his thoughts on the matter as follows: "I think that I have understood what you are saying, but it does not seem to be substantiated by the teachings of theology. Generally speaking, God does not give revelations through material devices. Perhaps you were a bit confused at the time when all this happened." In dealing with psychotic delusions, one can be definite and at the same time sympathetic. As a rule, it is extremely difficult to establish rapport with the psychotic, since he usually experiences alienation from other people, the religious counselor being no exception.[7] Arguing about the unreasonableness of the delusion can lead to endless bickering. The counselor should state his views and expect that the psychotic will immediately reject and refute them. Once this has happened, the counselor should merely say "I don't see it that way" and go no further.

The religious counselor should use all his ingenuity to lead the psychotic into a willingness to accept psychiatric help—and this is a very difficult thing to accomplish. Most psychotics have no insight into their mental state and consider themselves as normal as the next fellow. If the counselor fails in his attempt to get the psychotic to a psychiatrist, he should not feel discouraged. Many a psychiatrist has failed in the same endeavor. The better the counselor can understand the psychotic's frame of reference, the better are his chances for convincing him to accept treatment. Reading about the subjective aspects of psychosis can help the counselor gain some insight into this illness.

Many psychotics have a vague feeling that there is something amiss in their mental and emotional life, but they do not want to admit it to themselves. Sometimes success in getting the psychotic to treatment can be achieved through an appeal to this feeling. In trying to help the wife of the psychotic we have just described, the first step is to bring her to a realization that her husband is a sick person in need of psychiatric treatment. Often relatives are loath to admit that a person dear to them is insane. The stigma placed on mental illness by society makes them look upon it as a disgrace. Until this wife can recognize and accept her husband's condition, she will not be able to help him. Since as his wife she has become part of his delusional system, she will have little chance of convincing him that he needs psychiatric treatment. He would probably interpret her action as an attempt to get rid of him. She can be instrumental, however, in getting her husband to the family physician, who could make a medical referral for further psychiatric care. In some instances, the psychotic resists all efforts to get him into treatment and persists in his abnormal, disruptive behavior; in this case commitment to a mental hospital may be necessary. Commitment generally requires the consent of a close relative. Often a husband or wife is repelled by the thought of signing commitment papers, even when it is evident that this is the only course of action left. The religious counselor who has some understanding of psychosis can sometimes be helpful in convincing the relative that commitment is best for the psychotic. He can point out that this is the only way for the psychotic to regain his mental equilibrium.

The Neurotic Personality

Jane H., an unmarried woman of twenty-eight, comes to her pastor because she is unable to pray and is afraid she is losing her faith. Up to this time she has always been able to pray, and when troubled or anxious she has often found consolation in prayer. During the past few months she has gradually come to feel that her prayer is meaningless; she has tried to use other forms of prayer but nothing comes from the heart. In addition, she has been waking up each morning earlier and earlier and has not been able to go back to sleep. When she tries to pray during these periods she cannot. She has tried attending daily mass in hope of finding assistance, but this too is dry and empty. Religion has ceased to be of interest to her. She expresses concern over her constant fatigue and lack of interest in anything. She says she does not feel like doing anything but forces herself to act as usual to avoid worrying anyone, especially her parents, with whom she lives. The last few evenings while returning home from work on the bus she has found tears coming into her eyes and this greatly distresses her. She is unable to see any reason why she should feel so miserable much of the time. She admits having occasional thoughts of committing suicide. She is afraid that if she actually does lose her faith, she might follow through on a suicidal impulse.

This case illustrates some subjective experiences of the neurotic personality. The young woman demonstrates a clear need for psychotherapy as well as for the concern of her pastor. Her religious problem stems from her neurosis; before she can be assisted spiritually, she must receive psychological help. Exhortation to increased fidelity in prayer and devotion can only cause greater distress, as she has already tried this and failed. Depression and apathy have attacked most aspects of her everyday life—including religious belief and practice. She needs to deal with these pathological reactions before she can regain her faith. The religious counselor is equipped to handle normal religious doubts but not neurotic ones. The treatment of a neurosis is the proper concern of the psychiatrist or clinical psychologist. The religious counselor should bring to the counselee's awareness the emotional nature of her disorder and then make a good referral. Once the neurosis is lessened, the concern about faith will probably fade into the background and religion will gain its former meaning.

The Psychopathic Personality

John B. is a former seminarian, aged thirty-two. He is known at his parish rectory as an unstable alcoholic who abuses his wife and neglects his three children. His is an affable, outgoing person, well liked by anyone who has only a casual acquaintance with him. Most of the time he seems cheerful and carefree, even in the most pressing circumstances. He is a salesman who has frequently changed companies. He often gives the impression that he is on the verge of closing a $10,000 deal. Actually, he is such a poor provider that his wife works to support the children. He comes and goes pretty much as he pleases, sometimes being away from home as much as a week at a time. His wife knows that he has had affairs with other women, but she is determined to maintain some semblance of family life and so rejects any thought of separation. He is capable of flying into a rage for little apparent reason. Recently his ten-year-old son tracked some mud into the kitchen after playing ball in a vacant lot. John became furious and gave the boy a terrible beating. This incident precipitated the wife's coming to the rectory for advice.

Perhaps the most outstanding characteristic of this individual in his total lack of concern for anyone but himself.[8] He feels little guilt or remorse when he brings grief to his wife and children. This lack of guilt and concern poses a special problem for the religious counselor. When a person experiences anxiety, he is usually willing to take some steps to rid himself of it. The psychopath appears to be devoid of such distressing feelings, even in situations when his level of anxiety should be high. As a consequence, the religious counselor cannot appeal to inner distress to motivate change. When the counselor suggests psychiatric treatment, he may well meet with the retort, "What for? I'm not crazy." The only thing that the counselor can do is to point out that the psychopath's unusual behavior is seriously disrupting to other people, and even then the psychopath may not see how his behavior is unusual or disruptive. Such a person will sometimes accept help only when he is forced into it by circumstances—for example, if he is arrested for child neglect or drunken driving and ordered to see a psychiatrist by the court. Under these circumstances, treatment is sometimes quite ineffective and the psychopath continues to live as he did in the past. It is essential that the religious counselor understand the nature of this disorder and the psychopath's mental distortions if he is to help both the psychopath himself and his family. As we previously indicated, the counselor should guard against being manipulated to further the psychopath's ends. It is not beyond the psychopath to play the clergyman against the judge. Furthermore, he needs to be realistic in counseling those who are forced to cope with the psychopath's behavior, like his family. Even with the best treatment, success is limited.[9] The religious counselor trying to steer the psychopath into treatment can expect to fail as often as he succeeds, but he should realize that the failure usually stems from the nature of the disorder. He should not let frustration and discouragement get the better of him.

Making the Referral

Let us now turn to the problem of referring individuals to psychiatrists and psychologists. One of the functions of the religious counselor, as we have stated, is to aid people with everyday problems. In most cases, the counselor is equipped to offer effective help. He will encounter a few people, however, who are so disturbed and whose problems are so complex that they require a type of professional service beyond his training.

When one must deal with individuals who have emotional or mental disturbances screening can be a most vexing problem. The counselor must decide whom he should accept for counseling and whom he should refer to a psychiatrist or a psychologist. With the obviously psychotic or severely neurotic person, the decision is relatively simple. Disorders such as these are outside the scope of the religious counselor. The individual who is perplexed by every-day problems also offers little difficulty. The individual who is somewhat neurotic presents the greatest dilemma. The counselor must evaluate such a person's problem and decide whether he can help him.

After a few years of religious counseling, one usually discovers his capacities and limitations. He becomes proficient in recognizing people who have severe mental health problems. He learns from experience which individuals he can help and which he cannot. From this experience he can determine whether he is able to offer effective aid to a particular neurotic person.

Several other factors affect the counselor's acceptance or referral of a person. First and perhaps most important is the time he has available. If a religious counselor is to fulfill his assignment adequately he must make the best use of his time. Inevitably more people will seek help than he has time to offer; he cannot be tied down to a schedule limiting his services to a few disturbed individuals whom he sees weekly or even more frequently over a long period of time. The competent religious counselor offers the best possible service to the maximum number of people. This principle will ordinarily demand short-term counseling.

As a rule people who are quite disturbed or who have complex personality problems make slow progress in treatment calling for weekly interviews. They need to be seen twice a week or even more frequently.[10] The religious counselor who concentrates his effort upon a few neurotic individuals cannot do justice to all the other people who seek his help in solving less perplexing problems.

The expense of treatment is another factor in deciding on the final disposition of a case. Psychotherapy can be a very costly experience. Often a person is unable to meet the fees for private psychiatric treatment. A religious counselor, however, should not allow this obstacle to arouse his sympathy and guilt so that he eventually accepts the responsibility of trying to help someone whom he is inadequately trained to treat. Frequently counselees with financial need can use clinical facilities offered in a community. Most clinics set their fees on the basis of the patient's ability to pay. The religious counselor should become acquainted with the various psychiatric and psychological clinics in his area, the basis on which they accept patients, and the length of their waiting list.

Once the decision to refer a counselee to some outside source has been reached the next question that presents itself is "to whom should he be sent?" The answer frequently depends on the seriousness of the disorder. Often mental illness has a physical as well as a psychological effect.[11] This is particularly true in instances of severe illness. Consequently a very disturbed counselee should probably be referred to a psychiatrist for treatment. The psychiatrist can administer both medical treatment, such as drug or shock therapy, and psychotherapy. All psychiatrists are physicians and therefore can prescribe drugs for their patients. They also have considerable knowledge about the part shock therapies play in the treatment of the mentally ill. Their most intensive training, however, is in the field of psychotherapy. A psychiatrist's skill in handling both the medical therapies and psychotherapy is a good measure of his competence. An important part of his practice is diagnosis and choice of the most suitable therapy for a particular case. Therefore when an individual is severely disturbed by a disorder whose nature is still in doubt, he should be referred to a psychiatrist.

There are some mental and emotional illnesses which other professional personnel are equally well qualified to treat. Clinical psychologists more and more often undertake psychotherapy.[12] Intensive training in personality dynamics prepares them to understand the workings of the human mind. Supervised experience in psychotherapy equips them to be effective therapists. In addition to the psychologists, some social workers are also practicing psychotherapy. For the most part, their services are performed in a clinic under the guidance of a psychiatrist. Many psychologists also work as auxiliaries to psychiatrists. This arrangement is not always in effect, however. Some psychologists devote their time exclusively to private practice. Since psychologists do not have medical training, they limit themselves to patients whose mental and emotional disturbances do not involve physical disorders.

In general, psychiatrists treat the more severe cases of mental and emotional illness, and psychologists and psychiatric social workers treat the less severe. Therefore counselees who show signs of psychosis, such as hallucinations, fixed delusions, or suicidal tendencies, should be referred to a psychiatrist. The severely neurotic person may do well with either a psychiatrist or a psychologist. The competence of the therapist is usually the deciding factor. Complicated problems in social or vocational adjustment and severe speech or reading handicaps are the proper concern of clinical psychologists. Environmental difficulties involving interpersonal relationships, as in broken homes, are often best handled by social workers. If an individual is referred to a psychiatric or psychological clinic, the type of therapy and choice of therapist is left to the discretion of the staff. In this case the religious counselor is relieved of the difficult problem of deciding on the most suitable source of help for a particular case.

The Therapist's Religion

One of the problems which confronts the religious counselor is whether a counselee should be sent to a psychiatrist or psychologist of his own faith. Since there are few Catholic psychiatrists or psychologists in most communities and they are consequently greatly overworked, this problem can be extremely pressing. Because of the close relationship between psychiatry and religion, many people cling to the conviction that it would be immoral to accept treatment from a psychotherapist who is not of their own religious persuasion.[13] They base their conviction on the belief that such contact will make them lose their faith or will undermine their moral values.

A good psychotherapist accepts his patients completely, including their religious views and moral values. He does not force his religious views on them. If he thinks that the patient has a false view of his religious standards, he sends him to a religious counselor. If the patient has failed to live up to these standards, he may point out this inconsistency without condemning it. Thus, if a psychiatrist or a psychologist is truly skilled in his practice, he will do no harm to the faith of his patients.

Unfortunately, some irreligious psychiatrists and psychologists have entered the realm of religion and morals and as a result have caused considerable psychological and spiritual harm to their patients. Inevitably there are poor psychiatrists and psychologists, just as there are poor obstetricians and marriage counselors. This does not mean that we should condemn psychiatrists and psychologists who have no particular religious affiliation; instead we should investigate the proficiency of the professional therapist to whom we send counselees. Being religious does not make a therapist a good psychiatrist or psychologist, nor does claiming to be a Catholic or a Protestant make him a good member of his faith. If there is a choice between two equally competent therapists, one of whom holds the same religious convictions as the patient and one of whom does not, it would be better to choose the former. This referral is better not because the other therapist presents a threat to religious or moral integrity, but because the therapist of the same faith is likely to have a better understanding of the patient.

Basically, the problem of whether to refer the counselee to a psychiatrist of his own religion is solved by the counselor's knowledge of the therapist's skill and integrity. If the therapist with no religious affiliation has proven himself to be competent, there will be little danger of his undermining the faith or morals of the counselee. If investigations show that in the past he has harmed the religious and moral convictions of his patient, he is incompetent and as undeserving of a referral as an unskilled surgeon. On the other hand, it would be better to send a counselee to a proficient nonreligious psychiatrist who has some understanding of the faith than to a religious one who is lacking in professional competence.

The Relationship between Clergyman and Psychiatrist

The best way to evaluate a therapist's proficiency is to know him on a personal basis. In keeping with the spirit of dialogue characteristic of our era, clergymen have recently had many more contacts with psychiatrists and psychologists than formerly. In some cities, regular group discussions have contributed to mutual understanding and respect between the two professions. Even more encouraging are the professional and personal relationships that have in many instances resulted from these meetings. The clergyman has come to know the psychiatrist and vice versa. They have exchanged views and differences and have grown to like and respect each other. These relationships have often facilitated the effectiveness of the clergyman and the psychiatrist in assisting patients. It is a good idea for a religious counselor to establish several such friendships with psychiatrists and psychologists, since this is the best means of guaranteeing that he is referring the counselee to a competent, trustworthy person.

Making a Successful Referral

Achieving results smoothly and quickly in psychotherapy frequently depends upon the attitude of the patient. This attitude is usually formed before the patient ever enters the psychiatrist's or psychologist's office. One function of the counselor should be to try to offset in the counselee any negative attitudes that might hinder treatment.

For many people, the suggestion that they see a psychiatrist has but one meaning, that another individual has judged them to be "crazy." This is the usual reaction of those who are uninformed. The religious counselor frequently encounters this attitude and must correct it before the counselee will accept psychiatric help.

Psychiatry is a branch of medicine concerned with the mentally ill. Psychotherapy, one of its major tools, is a more intensive form of counseling. As a matter of fact, counseling and psychotherapy are so closely allied that it is often difficult to determine where one ends and the other begins. The degrees of mental illness are almost infinite, like the degrees of physical illness. One of the principal aims of psychiatric treatment is to deal with a neurotic or psychotic condition before it becomes serious. If the religious counselor can convey to the counselee some of these ideas, he may be able to lessen his anxiety about undergoing treatment.

Success or failure in convincing an individual to accept treatment frequently depends upon the attitude of the counselor. If the counselor has the mistaken idea that there is something degrading and humiliating about psychiatric care, he will probably convey this attitude to the counselee. On the other hand, if he has a clear idea of the function of a psychiatrist or psychologist and a positive attitude toward these professions, he will have won half the battle.

One of the prerequisites for successful psychotherapy is that the patient must want the therapy. Some counselees are aware of the seriousness of their disorder and willingly accept the suggestion of treatment; others who have less anxiety about their condition have little motivation for treatment. The counselor investigates the individual's desire for psychotherapy and strengthens it as much as possible. A half hour spent doing this may well determine the success of therapy.

It should be kept in mind, however, that there are some individuals who are mentally ill but unable to profit from treatment or to make further gains. There are mental as well as physical illnesses that cannot be cured or further ameliorated. For some people, borderline functioning is the best that can be achieved. People may consider them odd and different, but if they manage to get by there is little purpose in pressing for better adjustment. If the counselee has already undergone prolonged psychiatric treatment or reports that he has seen several psychiatrists, it is probable that another referral would be of little value. In this situation, the counselor's task is to care for the religious welfare of the counselee as best as he can under the circumstances. Perhaps through interest and concern he can help the counselee maintain his minimum psychological balance.

Dispelling False Ideas

The religious counselor can also help the abnormal counselee by giving him some idea of how psychotherapy proceeds. Frequently, this may merely entail dispelling false conceptions about psychotherapy. Many people have the erroneous notion that the psychiatrist or psychologist tells a patient what he must do and in a short time the disorder disappears if the patient does what he is told. Actually the patient does most of the work and the psychiatrist gives little advice. Under the direction of a therapist the patient probes the depths of his personality and thus comes to a better understanding of himself. He can then alter faulty emotional patterns and habitual reactions to certain situations. The change, however, must come from within the patient; the psychiatrist does not change him. During the initial interviews, most patients are somewhat baffled by the inactivity of the therapist. This stage of initial confusion may be prevented somewhat if the patient has been forewarned that he will do most of the work himself and that there is no pat advice to cure him in a few weeks.

The religious counselor who becomes skilled in referring individuals for psychiatric or psychological treatment earns the gratitude of both the individual and the therapist. He does much to make the trying journey back to sound mental health easier and more comfortable.

After the religious counselor has made a successful referral, his obligations to the counselee have not ended. Hopefully, the counselee remains a religious person during the process of psychiatric or psychological treatment. He still needs his relationship with God. The religious counselor should help the individual in psychiatric treatment derive the greatest possible benefit from his religious affiliation. This may mean occasional visits with the religious counselor during the course of therapy to strengthen the religious commitment. At this time doubts about religion can be discussed as well as possible areas of conflict between religion and psychiatry. The continuing relationship with the religious counselor can have great significance to the counselee and hasten the time when he no longer needs psychiatric or psychological care.

Conclusion

Looking back over the discussions in this chapter and the previous ones, we realize that religious counseling, like all kinds of counseling, is a dialogue. But it is a specialized one. Its primary goal is to make the counselee more aware of the spiritual dimensions of the problem he is confronted with. How well the dialogue progressed depends greatly on the type of relationship established between the "speakers."

If the counselee senses understanding and acceptance from his counselor, then he feels that he is dealing with someone he can trust; consequently he is better able to tackle his dilemma. Even in cases in which the difficulty is so complex and confusing that the counselee is unable to begin to resolve his problem, having a good rapport with the counselor makes him at least receptive to possible solutions that will be suggested during the talks.

Often the selection of the best alternative depends on the counselee's being aware of God's speaking to him—both inside and outside the counseling sessions. Such a realization can be achieved only if the counselee has gained some peace of mind through the feeling of trust he has found in the counseling relationship thus far. Only then will he *want* to try to resolve his difficulties through the counseling experience.

References

[1] Gordon W. Allport, *Pattern and Growth in Personality* (New York: Holt, Rinehart & Winston, Inc., 1961), pp. 150–51.

[2] The Committee on Nomenclature and Statistics of the American Psychiatric Association, *Diagnostic and Statistical Manual: Mental Disorders* (Washington, D.C.: American Psychiatric Association, 1952).

[3] Thomas W. Klink, *Clergyman's Guide to Recognizing Serious Mental Illness* (New York: The National Association for Mental Health, *circa* 1954).

[4] James C. Coleman, *Abnormal Psychology and Modern Life* (Chicago: Scott, Foresman & Company, 1964).

[5] A. A. Terruwe, *Psychopathic Personality and Neurosis* (New York: P. J. Kenedy & Sons, 1958).

[6] Robert W. White, *The Abnormal Personality* (New York: The Ronald Press Company, 1964).

[7] Benjamin B. Wolman, "Schizophrenia and Related Disorders," in *Handbook of Clinical Psychology*, ed. B. Wolman (New York: McGraw-Hill Book Company, 1965).

[8] S. K. Weinberg, *Society and Personality Disorder* (New York: Prentice-Hall, Inc., 1952), pp. 264–69.

[9] *Ibid.*, pp. 269–70.

[10] Lewis R. Wolberg, *The Technique of Psychotherapy*, Part I (New York: Grune & Stratton, Inc., 1967), pp. 510–11.

[11] Coleman, *op. cit.*, pp. 285–310.

[12] Irving E. Alexander, "Post-Doctoral Training in Clinical Psychology," in *Handbook of Clinical Psychology*, ed. B. Wolman (New York: McGraw-Hill Book Company, 1965).

[13] R. P. Vaughan, "Referring Students to Psychiatrists and Psychologists," *The Catholic Counselor*, III (1959), 34–37.

Suggested Bibliography

Arbuckle, Dugald S., *Counseling: An Introduction*. Boston: Allyn & Bacon, Inc., 1961.

Bordin, E., *Psychological Counseling*. New York: Appleton-Century-Crofts, 1955.

Cavanagh, J. R., *Fundamental Pastoral Psychology*. Milwaukee, Wis.: The Bruce Publishing Co., 1962.

Cottle, W. C., and Downie, N. M., *Procedures and Preparations for Counseling*. Englewood Cliffs, N. J.: Prentice-Hall, Inc., 1960.

Curran, Charles A., *Counseling in Catholic Life and Education*. New York: The Macmillan Company, 1952.

Godin, André, S. J., *The Pastor as Counselor*. New York: Holt, Rinehart & Winston, Inc., 1965.

Hagmaier, G., and Gleason, R., *Counseling the Catholic*. New York: Sheed and Ward, 1959.

Hiltner, S., *Pastoral Counseling*. Nashville, Tenn.: Abingdon Press, 1950.

Hostie, Raymond, S. J., *Pastoral Counseling*. New York: Sheed and Ward, 1966.

May, Rollo, *The Art of Counseling*. New York: Abingdon-Cokesbury, 1939.

158

Patterson, C. H., *Counseling and Guidance in Schools*. New York: Harper & Row, Publishers, 1962.

Porter, E. H., *Introduction to Therapeutic Counseling*. Boston: Houghton Mifflin Company, 1950.

Rogers, Carl R., *Client-Centered Therapy*. Boston: Houghton Mifflin Company, 1959.

———, *On Becoming a Person*. Boston: Houghton Mifflin Company, 1961.

Snyder, William., *Casebook of Non-Directive Counseling*. Boston: Houghton Mifflin Company, 1950.

Tyler, Leona E., *The Work of the Counselor*. New York: Appleton-Century-Crofts, 1953.

Vanderveldt, J., and Odenwald, R., *Psychiatry and Catholicism* (2nd ed.). New York: McGraw-Hill Book Company, 1957.

Van Kaam, Ardian, *The Art of Existential Counseling*. Wilkes-Barre, Pa.: Dimension Books, 1966.

Williamson, E. G., *Counseling Adolescents*. New York: McGraw-Hill Book Company, 1950.

Index